JUNGLE DIVE-BOMBERS
AT WAR

JUNGLE DIVE-BOMBERS AT WAR

Peter C. Smith

JOHN MURRAY

© Peter C. Smith 1987

First published 1987
by John Murray (Publishers) Ltd
50 Albemarle Street, London W1X 4BD

Typeset by Inforum Ltd, Portsmouth
Printed and bound in Great Britain
at the Bath Press, Avon

British Library CIP Data
Smith, Peter C. (Peter Charles, *1940*–).
Jungle dive-bombers at war.
1. World war, 1939–1945 —— Aerial
operations   2. World war, 1939–1945 ——
Campaigns —— Pacific Ocean   3. Dive
bombers —— History
I. Title
940.54'4   D785

ISBN 0–7195–4425–4

CONTENTS

Introduction		1
1	Early Development of Dive-Bombing	3
2	Pearl Harbor to Salween Gorge	13
3	Rabaul and Guadalcanal	33
4	Counter-Strike	54
5	Across the Imphal	72
6	The Secret Squadrons	89
7	New Zealand's Special Squadron	105
8	No Place to Hide	126
9	The Philippines Regained	144
	Epilogue	160
	Sources	173
	Index	177

ILLUSTRATIONS

between pages 86 and 87

1 US Marine Corps Major Ross 'Rusty' Rowell flew DH–4 aircraft in Nicaragua, 1927
2 A Curtiss P–40 fighter of the famous 'Flying Tigers'
3 Japanese naval aircrew at Rabaul, 1942, before their special mission against New Guinea
4 Japanese troops in front of a D3A1 'Val' at an airbase in the Philippines
5 A Japanese 'Val' dive-bomber on a combat mission, *c.* September 1942
6 Ditched and abandoned Aichi D3A1 on the beach at Table Bay, Papua, September 1942
7 An Australian Vultee Vengeance of No 12 Squadron RAAF in camouflaged revetment
8 Australian Vultee Vengeances returning to Nadzab after another strike at Japanese positions on the north coast of New Guinea, 1944
9 Australian Vultee Vengeance dive-bombers of No 12 Squadron RAAF
10 Australian navigator Ron Gabrielson of No 84 Squadron RAF in Burma
11 Underview of a bomb-bay of an Australian Vultee Vengeance of No 12 Squadron RAAF
12 W/Cdr Arthur Murland Gill of No 84 Squadron RAF who used a Spitfire, nicknamed 'The Looker', to carry out reconnaissance sorties ahead of dive-bomber strikes
13 A full wing strike against a Japanese-held village in the Imphal plain is led by No 84 Squadron RAF, May 1944
14 Silhouette of a Vultee Vengeance over the Burmese jungle
15 The US Navy Construction Battalions ('Seebees') at work preparing a temporary airstrip
16 SBD5 Dauntless dive-bombers of No 25 Squadron RNZAF on Bougainville island
17 Typical pre-briefing mission for a US Marine Corps dive-bomber unit

18 A US Marine Corps SBD5 heads back to base across the mountain ranges of New Britain

19 US Marine Corps dive-bombers attack ammunition dumps and AA-batteries on Bougainville island

20 S/Ldr T. J. MacLean de Lange who led No 25 Squadron RNZAF during the Bougainville campaign with such success

21 New Zealand Dauntless flights lead another mass strike against the Japanese on Rabaul, 1944

22 A SBD5 of No 25 Squadron RNZAF flies low over Japanese-held New Britain searching out fresh targets

23 A Japanese Yokosuka D4Y, 'Judy'

24 Japanese navy ground crew working on a Yokosuka D4Y, 'Judy'

25 A gaggle of Curtiss SB-2C Helldivers returns to Task Force 58 after missions over Saipan in late 1944

26 The classic pose of the Curtiss SB-2C Helldiver with bomb-doors open

27 The Air Commando units of the USAAF were set up in north Assam in support of General Stilwell's forces and Merrill's Marauders

28 A Mustang pilot of the composite Chinese/American wing examines flak damage to his aircraft

29 Indo-China, 1954: a French patrol moves into a village near Dien Bien Phu to 'mop up' in the wake of a dive-bombing attack

30 French navy Helldivers on patrol over the Tonkin delta, 1954

31 Helldivers of the French navy's 3 Flotille d'Assault lined up at Bach Mai airbase near Hanoi, April 1954

32 A target's-eye view of a Douglas Dauntless with its distinctive 'cheese-grater' dive-brakes lowered

ILLUSTRATION SOURCES

1, 2, 25, 26, 27, 28: US National Archives, Washington, DC; 3, 5, 6: Robert & Misako Piper; 4: Tadashi Nozawa; 7, 8: Australian War Memorial; 9: Cyril J. McPherson; 10: Ron Gabrielson; 11: Royal Australian Air Force; 12, 13, 14: Arthur M. Gill; 15, 16, 18, 19, 20, 21, 22: Meg Campbell; 23, 24: Author's Collection; 29, 32: ECP Armées, Paris; 30, 31: H. de Lestapis

MAPS

1 Western Pacific and Indian Ocean combat area, 1941–8 pp. 14/15

2 Strategic locations of SW Asia, Dec. 1941   46/47

ACKNOWLEDGEMENTS

In a book of this nature 90 per cent of the work is like an iceberg – under the surface. This involves years of research and the tracking down of obscure leads in many countries – of which the reader sees only the end-result, often cut down and changed. No such work can be done by a historian on his own and this book is certainly no exception. Among the many people who were kind enough to give me generous help when I requested it I would like to thank the following: Dale Birdsell, Chief Historian, Department of the Army, Alexandria, Virginia; Mrs Jeannette E. Bridler, University of Texas at El Paso, Texas; John Bright-Holmes, for tactfully curbing my worst excesses at the word-processor; Meg Campbell, of Wellington, New Zealand; B. F. Cavalcante, Navy Historical Center, Washington, DC; George G. Chalou and John Mendellsohn, Military Archives Division, US National Archives, Washington, DC; Danny J. Crawford, Head, Reference Section, HQ United States Marine Corps, Washington, DC; Curator, ECPA Armées, Vincennes, France; Curator SIRPA Fort d'Ivry, Paris; F. R. Dyer, Ryde, IOW; Mrs and the late Ron Gabrielson, Hope Valley, South Australia; Wesley B. Henry, Research Division, Wright-Patterson AFB, Ohio, USA; Captain Claude Huan, Paris; George Isaacs, Wembley Park, London; Roger A. Jernigan, Office of Air Force History, Bolling AFB, Washington, DC; Douglas Johnstone; Captain H. de Lestapis, Paris; Wing Commander Arthur Murland Gill, Llanwarne, Hereford; Colonel Elmer Glidden, Canton, Massachusetts, USA; T. G. Hansford, Wells, Somerset; Bud McInnes; Air Commodore T. J. MacLean de Lange, Rotorua, New Zealand; Cyril J. McPherson; Robert C. Mikesh and Norman G. Richards, NASM, Smithsonian Institution, Washington, DC; Douglas Morris, Parkstone, Poole, Dorset; Tadashi Nozawa, Tokyo;

Judy Peeples, Defense Audiovisual Agency, Washington, DC; Robert and Misako Piper, RAAF Historical Section, Canberra; John Ramsden, Berrick Salome, Oxford; George Ravenscroft, Kensington, London; Donald J. Ritchie; Commander Sadao Seno Kanagawa-ken, Japan; Ken R. Scadden, National Archives, Department of Internal Affairs, Wellington, New Zealand; Major Lester A. Sliter, USAF Historical Research Center, Maxwell AFB, Alabama; Lt-Colonel R. B. Tiffany, History and Museums Division, HQ US Marine Corps, Washington, DC; Ken Tonkin, Rosslyn Park, South Australia; H. Widdop, Halifax; Richard A. von Doenhoff, Navy and Old Army Branch, Military Archives Division, NARS, Washington, DC; and, finally, my special thanks to the Chief Librarian and his most helpful staff at the Central Library, Harpur Street, Bedford, who have always been exceedingly helpful in meeting my requests for rare books and documents from obscure sources.

Peter C. Smith
Riseley, Bedford
April 1987

INTRODUCTION

The use of the dive-bomber for attaining the necessary and vital accuracy to hit and destroy small or obscured 'pinpoint' targets has seldom been shown to such good effect as in the jungle campaigns, particularly of the Second World War. In such campaigns the over-riding need for accuracy in close support of ground forces has been proven over and over again, in particular in operations in South-East Asia, most recently in Vietnam.

Many groups and people have laid claim to having originated dive-bombing, but the most convincing is that of the fledgling Royal Air Force and its immediate predecessor, the Royal Flying Corps. They conducted the most detailed research into the technique of the close support of troops on the ground and applied it successfully in combat in 1917 and 1918. Dive-bombing as a separate technique, as part of the close-support concept, was first used in combat by British flyers in 1917, and the first detailed and scientific tests into its applications a year later. Among the earliest American advocates of these methods was 'Billy' Mitchell, whose predictions in the early 1920s about the effectiveness of dive-bombing were later forgotten when he turned to the Heavy Bomber concept for the expansion of the US Army Air Corps. He was then following the same principle of 'strategic' rather than 'tactical' warfare as propounded by, among others, Lord Trenchard, the head of the RAF, in Britain and General Douhet in Italy.

The irony in the story of dive-bombing is that the service which did most to keep alive the technique in the 1920s, and which brought it to perfection in 1945, was the US Marine Corps. Yet the Marine Corps owed much of the credit to the Army Air Corps for introducing them to the concept.

Precision necessitated the special skill and accuracy of the dive-bomber, and this was just as true of targets in Spain in

1937, in Poland in 1939, and in France and the Soviet Union in 1940 and 1941 respectively, as it was in the naval battles of the Pacific War between 1941-5. But these applications – whether by German Stuka, Soviet Peshka, British Skua or Japanese Suisei planes – have no place in this book. Those battles and achievements have been described elsewhere. This book approaches the war in the Pacific from a very different viewpoint to the one with which most British readers have been familiar hitherto: it studies dive-bombing in relation to jungle targets where pinpoint accuracy was even more necessary than in conventional fighting. For completeness, however, the very first instance of a jungle dive-bomber campaign is included; as is one of the lesser known post-war instances when French navy dive-bombers were used at Dien Bien Phu. I hope, therefore, that this fresh insight into the dive-bomber story will provide a different perspective on the history of close-support combat aviation.

I
Early Development of Dive-Bombing

In order to understand the background of the application of dive-bombing to jungle warfare, it is necessary to examine the early precedents for such action before the outbreak of war between the USA, Great Britain and Japan in the Pacific in December 1941. These actions involved the US Marine Corps, took place on jungle-clad islands in the Caribbean, and concerned the same type of aircraft: the De Havilland DH–4 biplane – one that would hardly qualify as a dive-bomber in any air force.

The prototype of the DH–4 first flew in August 1916. It was the first aircraft designed specifically as a bomber for the British services, and it was a two-seat, single-engine biplane – typical of its period – of wooden construction and fabric covered, with a fixed undercarriage. Its power plant, varied typically by a machine fitted with a 250-hp Rolls-Royce Eagle III engine driving a four-bladed wooden propeller, was capable of a maximum speed of 119mph at 3000ft, and a service ceiling of 16,000ft. It was equipped to carry a pair of 230-lb bombs or four 112-lb bombs and was defensively armed with a twin, synchronised Vickers machine-gun firing forward and a single Lewis gun in the after-cockpit, firing astern. The DH–4s joined both the Royal Flying Corps and the Royal Naval Air Service and had a distinguished war record in 1917 and 1918; and it was certainly one of the best aircraft of the Frist World War.

Such was the expansion of the aerial arm of the services, however, that substantial subcontracting had to be entered into to produce the numbers required. As well as those built at the De Havilland Aircraft Manufacturing Company's Hendon

plant in north London, others were built by F. W. Berwick,
Vulcan Motor & Engineering, and Westland Aircraft in Great
Britain. When the United States entered the war in 1917 with
her vast manufacturing and labour resources, further subcontracting for aircraft took place on a large scale, and this included
the DH-4.

British flyers employed the DH-4A in a dive-bombing role,
and one pilot commented on how, because of the lack of air
brakes, speed built up in the attack dive. Many of the American
pilots who fought in Europe had closely observed British
techniques on the Western Front. Against small targets, lightly
protected by anti-aircraft fire, the best technique that had been
worked out was to dive directly at the target and to release the
bombs at the point of pull-out. This proved by far the most
accurate method of delivering bombs on to such targets and was
widely copied.

By 1919, before production was halted, no less that 4846
DH-4As had been built for America. Suddenly the Americans
found themselves with numbers of unwanted light bombers for
which they had little use. Moreover they were semi-obsolete for
an improved version, the DH-4B had been produced and the
US Marine Corps was an early customer. Under their designation O2B-1 some thirty M-1s were built by Boeing. They had
a speed of 118mph and a range of 330 miles. They were fitted
with a single 0.30in. calibre machine-gun in the after-cockpit.

The first testing of a primitive dive-bombing technique
against a jungle target took place in Haiti. In 1915 the US
Marines had landed there, under the aegis of the Monroe
Doctrine, to restore order during a period of internal unrest.
They were still in Haiti four years later when among their
contingent the 4th Air Squadron, commanded by Captain
Harvey B. Mims, landed at Port-au-Prince and was sent into
action against bands of Caco rebels.

After several unsuccessful attempts to cause damage or
casualties to groups hidden deep in the interior jungle by using
conventional level-bombing methods, one Marine flyer,
Lieutenant L. H. Sanderson, decided to utilise a diving attack.
The problem, however, was a method of bomb release that

would not be more dangerous to his aircraft than to the rebels. His solution was a novel one. A large canvas sack, normally used for carrying mail but strong enough to contain one of the light bombs of the period, was attached to the fuselage. A draw rope then tied this to the rear cockpit and secured the bomb in a horizontal position for the flight to the target.

On sighting the rebels Sanderson put his aircraft into a 45-degree dive against the largest group in view and sped down to a height of only 250ft to make sure of his target. The draw rope was then released and the weight of the bomb was carried out and down by gravity and the momentum of the aircraft. The bomb cleared the propeller safely as Sanderson pulled out of the dive, and its explosion appeared to take place reasonably close to the centre of the rebel group. This primitive method was hailed as the first 'dive-bombing' attack. It was not, of course, but even so it probably was the first accurate dive-bombing of a target in a jungle context.

Back in the United States other pilots experimented with the idea. Lieutenant Lester B. Sweeley used a DH–4B equipped with a 300-lb bomb on a Mk XVI bomb rack to conduct one test at the Aberdeen Proving Ground in September 1919, diving to a height of 1000ft before releasing. But it was the actual combat application by the four squadrons of 3 Attack Group during their patrols along the Mexican border between 1919 and 1921 that most attracted the attention of Erastus 'Rusty' Rowell, a young US Marine Corps pilot, on assignment with 1 Pursuit (Fighter) Group, in 1923. This Group was commanded by Major Lewis H. Brereton (who as a Lieutenant-General was to command 1 Allied Airborne Army in Europe in the Second World War); and they had their DH–4s fitted with American type A–3 under-wing bomb racks and so would carry up to ten small bombs on each wing. The pilots were experienced flyers used to the terrain and they developed the refinement of having the bomb-release switch fitted inside the pilot's cockpit. This was essential for, in a diving attack, only the pilot could decide the precise point of release.

And this was the method they used. Despite the strain inflicted on these old aircraft they found they could dive on to

their target at quite a steep angle, 60–70 degrees being the
norm, and the DH–4's 'wires and struts' configuration would
keep the speed of the dive to acceptable limits, contrary to what
British pilots had reported in 1918. They would then line up the
target using normal eye-sighting, aided by any small projection
from the engine cowling to help them with alignment. The
results were not only impressively accurate but consistently so
too; and there had been no losses. It was against this background that the second, and far more influential, example of
the application of dive-bombing techniques to resolve a jungle
campaign began with a discussion between two young officers
at an airstrip close to the Mexican border. These were US
Army Air Corps Lieutenant 'Turk' Tourtellot and Erastus
Rowell. Both men were destined for distinguished careers in
their respective services, Tourtellot to rise to Brigadier-
General while Rowell became a Major-General of the Marine
Corps. Their historic meeting took place at Kelly Field, an
Army Air Service airbase at which 3 Attack Group was then
stationed.

Rowell stated that, although 'no one would believe that the
wing structure of that type of plane could withstand the strains
of dive-bombing' the accuracy they had achieved by such
methods, 'was most impressive to me and I immediately visual-
ised certain naval employment of such tactics where accuracy
against small moving targets is paramount'. But ultimately he
was to put the method to the test against land targets, and in the
jungle.

In the summer of 1924 Rowell's new posting found him in
command of Marine Squadron VO–1–M at San Diego air
station, the first Marine air formation to be based on the West
Coast. The unit again was equipped with DH–4Bs fitted with
the Liberty engine, and so he was able to implement the lessons
he had absorbed earlier. As counter-insurgency operations in
support of Marines on the ground, of the type that the Marine
Corps had undertaken in 1919 in Haiti, were on the cards for his
future employment Rowell considered that it would pay a
handsome dividend if he could duplicate their accuracy. The
squadron had just returned from participation in the American

occupation of Santo Domingo. His first task, after writing to Lieutenant Walter Peck to obtain sample assemblies of the remote-control gun gear, was to fix them to his aircraft with improvised pilot bomb-release switches just as the Army had done. Initially his DH-4Bs were fitted with small navy-type bomb racks. Later these bomb racks were upgraded by the acquisition, from the US Bureau of Aeronautics, of A-3 racks like those being used by the army but which were not yet navy issue. They could, however, carry the standard navy-type practice bombs. Rowell's men then made experimental bombing runs until they became very proficient at the new method.

Between serious applications most service units were in great demand all over the United States with the 'barnstorming' type of air shows. Exhibition flying was done with formations and smoke laying, but Rowell's Marines were now able to add a new facet to the standard show by combining dive-bombing with the use of smoke-bombs. This proved a star attraction at the shows and also accompanied the Dedication Ceremonies at the many new airfields being opened across the United States at this time. These shows spread the doctrine of the diving attack to a new generation and much influenced navy airmen. Inevitably, though, it was also at a later version of one of these dive-bombing displays that the German ace, Ernst Udet, first witnessed and was wholeheartedly converted to dive-bombing.

It was not long before Rowell's men were able to put their new-found skills to a more practical test. American forces had been established in Nicaragua, the largest of the Central American republics, since 1912. They not only remained there on and off for the next twenty years, but were instrumental in training up a National Guard to take their place. That presence was further established with the purchase of naval bases at Fonseca Bay, on the north-west coast, and Isla del Maiz, off the east coast, through the Bryan-Chamarre Treaty of February and June 1916. Although US Marines had been active in Nicaragua in the early 1920s, it was the uprising against the dictator Diaz in the middle of that decade that caused Rowell's Marines' involvement and the first jungle dive-bombing actions. Under the rebel leader, Moncada, the insurgents quickly spread through the hinterland of the country and, in January 1927, America dispatched the 5th Marines to stop the conflict and maintain a cease-fire between the two factions. The number of troops was found to be inadequate, but by early May they had been increased to brigade strength. Their job, away from the western coast and the main cities, was made difficult by the nature of the land and the scarcity of road and rail links. The majority of the population (90 per cent) then lived, and still does, in the narrow lowland belt on the eastern side of the country around the two lakes of Nicaragua and Managua. The climate is tropical, but a triangle of sheer mountain rises in the north, feeding numerous rivers and streams which run down on the Caribbean side into dense jungle and rain forests.

As so often happens in such circumstances, the Marine garrisons found themselves spread out in isolated points along the tenuous rail link. Obviously air support could lessen their reliance on the rail link, which could so easily be cut, and on the jungle tracks, which with mule transport meant that relief and supply columns took weeks to cover relatively short distances.

During the long period of negotiation, led by the US Government representative Henry Stimson, which finally led to the Armistice, VO–I–M received orders at short notice in mid-February 1927 to ship out from San Diego with its DH–4s and move into Nicaragua. Only a few days later, on 25 February, the unit was disembarking at the Nicaraguan port of Cortinto on the north-west coast. The seven aircraft were unshipped, their wings detached and all parts were loaded aboard flat trucks and hauled by rail down the coast to Managua. Working through the night, despite their weariness at the long journey, the Marine flyers had their base established at the baseball ground in a suburb of the capital and turned it into the nation's only airfield. All seven of their machines were re-assembled within forty-eight hours of disembarkation.

At this period so few Marines had arrived that it was the flyers alone who held the ring between the rival forces until the main ground force under Brigadier General Feland arrived from Quantico. The US Marines had secured the capital and some of the larger towns but other detachments were spread out in fourteen small garrisons along the vital north-south rail link. They were under strict instructions not to get involved against either combatant, unless they themselves were fired upon, and they performed this difficult duty with considerable restraint.

A second Marine air unit, VO–4–M, arrived as reinforcement for VO–1–M and, under Rowell's command, they formed the Marine Aircraft Squadron. The DH–4Bs flew continually on reconnaissance patrols, keeping watchful eyes on the movements of both armies in order to prevent any advantage being gained by one or the other while negotiations proceeded. Finally, in June 1927, the rival leaders signed the Armistice. The terms called for new elections to be held in 1928 which the United States promised to supervise in order to guarantee fair play (as it was to do also in 1930 and 1932). At this point, however, it seemed that their work was done and preparations for a withdrawal were under way. Rowell's force was therefore reduced and re-numbered VO–7–M.

One of the rebel commanders, Augusto Sandoni, more radical than the rest, could not stomach what he saw as the meek surrender of their cause and vowed to maintain the fight to the bitter end. Unilaterally he declared the Armistice null and void and took off with his immediate followers to continue the struggle in the mountains in the north. All the other troops of both sides had lain down their arms so he would have been in a strong position except for the US Marines.

One isolated Marine outpost was at Ocotal, some 125 miles in a direct line from the nearest friendly force, but 10–14 days away in practical terms of a relief column using mules. The garrison, commanded by Marine Captain Hatfield, had 37 Marines supplemented by about 50 men of the newly formed and freshly recruited Nicaraguan National Guard still being trained by a Marine NCO.

This small group was surprised on the evening of 15 July 1927, when Sandino attacked the town with a force estimated at 700–800 strong, fully armed. The two sections were cut off from each other by the open Town Plaza across which all movement became impossible and, although both sections reacted with vigour to a fierce attack made at 03.00 the next morning, they were isolated and doomed unless help could be brought quickly. A relief column of 65 Marines under Major Floyd had set off on receipt of a radio warning but they needed ten days to reach the garrison. Its position seemed very precarious.

Radio reports of the garrison's plight soon reached Rowell and by 10.10 the following morning two aircraft were circling the town of Ocotal. Despite the hazards one made a daring landing and established contact with Hatfield. The aircraft then survived a bumpy take-off to rejoin its companion and both machines returned to the capital to report Hatfield's detailed account to Rowell. All the available aircraft were soon airborne and heading to the rescue.

The use of the baseball field as an airstrip meant that only a 400-yard runway was available and that the DHs could not take off fully laden. Another limitation was the need to carry at least 110 gallons of fuel for the round-trip to Ocotal including time for an attack. So only a partial bomb-load could be carried by each aircraft.

After the long flight over jungle-clad hills the squadron approached the target area. A tropical storm was brewing, with black clouds building up ahead, and rain began to fall during the attack, which had to be made quickly, otherwise the mission would be abortive. Rowell first led his aircraft in a preliminary circuit over the enemy positions to locate their strongest concentrations, then he began the attack. Rowell later recalled:

> All the pilots had been trained in dive-bombing and that was the kind of attack that I planned to employ. As I made the approach on the town, we formed a bombing column. We were fired upon as we flew over the outposts along the river, but at 1500ft did not suffer any particular damage from rifle fire.
>
> I led off the attack and dived out of column from 1500ft, pulling out at about 600ft. Later we ended up by diving in from 1000ft and pulling out at about 300ft. Since the enemy had not been subjected to any form of bombing attack, other than the dynamite charges thrown from the Laird Swallows of the Nicaraguan Air Force, they had no fear of us. They exposed themselves in such a manner that we were able to inflict damage which was out of proportion to what they might have suffered had they taken cover.

With the accuracy inherent in the diving attack to low level, and unopposed by the enemy save for ineffectual rifle fire, the 17-lb fragmentation bombs dropped by the five DHs caused heavy losses and much confusion. It was hard to estimate from the air in the conditions prevailing, but the subsequent scattering of the enemy and the large numbers of bodies on the ground proved how effective the dive-bombing had been. It was calculated later that between 40–80 rebel soldiers were killed with up to 200 casualties in all. This was a devastating blow to the Sandoni forces who broke and fled the area; and it was a triumphant debut for the dive-bombers.

That unprepared troops should crack when subjected to such an apparently 'personal' attack from the air was not too surprising. The same effect had been found by British flyers at Nablus against the Turkish army and in the Kosturino Pass against the Bulgarian Army both on 21 September 1918, while the lesson had been repeated by Allied flyers on the Conegliano-Pordonone road against the Austro-Hungarian army a month later.

Now, with the siege lifted and his methods vindicated, Rowell was able to take his VO–7–M from strength to strength. The Marines on the ground called upon its services more and more as they pursued the rebels deeper in the mountains. Rowell wrote: 'This attack was highly successful and followed by a great many similar types of air action throughout the following two years. There was never an occasion when this form of air attack failed to disperse the enemy with losses.'

The campaign was a long and protracted one, for the mountains were difficult to breach and the enemy kept on the move. Finally, however, they established themselves in a strong fortress position atop Chipote mountain. Here they proved very difficult to root out. They could attack the straggling American columns as they approached and then melt away into the jungle again before they could be pinned down, the classic guerrilla tactic. Again the dive-bombers were called into action to provide the solution. According to Rowell:

There was another formation attack which I led. It consisted of only four planes because we were reduced to that number due to operational and normal casualties. It was one of the first occasions when we used the new Corsairs just received . . . In this attack we made the approach from down-wind over a layer of overcast clouds, and delivered the assault from almost vertical dives. This attack was also successful in inflicting losses and resulted in wide dispersal of the main body of the enemy. That was the first time we used the 50-lb demolition bombs.

The use of dive-bombing was now well established in the US Navy also and specialised aircraft were being designed to carry bombs of up to 500lb for use against the superstructures and exposed anti-aircraft positions of large warships, against the lighter destroyer-type warships, and against aircraft-carriers. But it was the Marines who had shown exactly how efficient this technique could be when used against difficult land targets, and against jungle-shrouded targets in particular.

What nobody knew, of course, was that, fifteen years on, a bloody and protracted war would have to be fought between the major powers in just such conditions, and that the jungle-clad hills and islands of forgotten or unknown lands would become the major stage for the ultimate expression of the dive-bombers' skills.

2
Pearl Harbor to Salween Gorge

During the 1930s the Imperial Japanese navy had observed the development of the dive-bomber in both Germany and the United States. Under the terms of the Washington naval convention of 1922, under which the nine signatory states undertook not to build more capital ships for ten years, the Japanese fleet had been frozen at about two-thirds the strength of the Royal Navy and the US Navy in terms of battleships and other warships. The Japanese resented this and, under air-minded commanders like Admiral Yamamoto, sought to redress the balance by alternative methods. The apparent ability of dive-bombing to hit targets much more often than other methods naturally aroused their interest and designs based on early German dive-bombers were ordered from the Heinkel company; while Japanese aviation engineers and test pilots soon produced quality aircraft of their own for dive-bombing.

Naturally it was as an anti-ship weapon that the dive-bomber was seen and developed in both the Japanese and US navies at this time but, during the long and arduous land campaign brought about by Japan's intervention on the Chinese mainland from 1931 onward, armies also came to realise the value of such a precision air weapon for close-support operations with the ground troops. Initially the Japanese army had no such aircraft in its armoury (both Japan and America organised its aircraft at this time as 'air arms' of the traditional forces, and not as a separate Air Force in its own right as was the case in Great Britain, even though there was also a Fleet Air Arm). Soon, however, the Japanese began developments on these lines, and the specification they laid down was one that has, in broad outline, remained the same for aircraft of this type right down

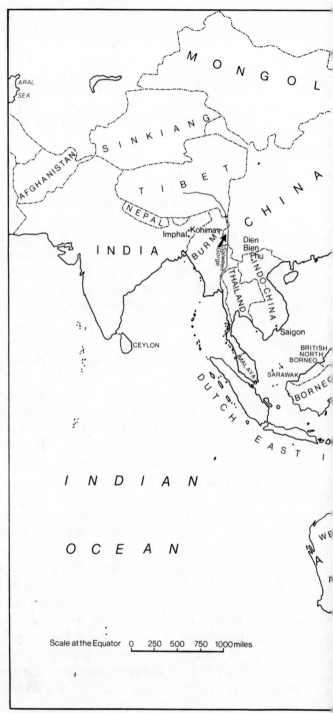

1 *The Western Pacific and Indian Ocean combat area, 19.*

to modern times. They asked for inexpensive, tough planes, able to operate from primitive and make-shift airstrips close to the front line. Because such aircraft were to serve in direct support of troops accuracy was needed above all else and only dive-bombing then provided such accuracy. This they proved time-and-time again in their expanding wars.

Traditionally the Japanese navy had provided much of the close support for such operations. Using early dive-bombers based on aircraft carriers out at sea the Japanese Fleet Air Arm had given direct dive-bombing aid to the Japanese Marines at Shanghai and such air support had been provided regularly since then. Thus a whole level of understanding of the needs for close support developed in the Navy. This was to pay a handsome dividend a few years later when ship-borne dive-bombers provided Japanese land forces, Army as well as Marines, with an expertise sadly lacking in the Allied fleets' air contingents other than the US Marine Corps flyers.

The Pacific War is usually remembered only for the period from December 1941, when the Japanese attacked Pearl Harbor, to August 1945, when they surrendered after the dropping of the atomic bombs on Hiroshima and Nagasaki; but China and Japan had been locked in combat for the better part of a decade. This bitter conflict was later to merge with the wider campaigns as the Japanese swept south but it all stemmed from the Mukden, or China, Incident of 1931. Japan herself had been invaded and exploited in the centuries before and had, as a consequence, retreated into isolation. It was when she was forced out into the modern world by the western nations in the mid-nineteenth century that she reawakened. Modern technology was thrust upon her, adapted by her and turned against her mentors. Flexing her new-found strength she took revenge by first penetrating, then annexing Korea, humiliating Russia in 1905 and then beginning her planned expansion, first into Manchuria, which she took over fully in 1931, and then making further encroachments upon the Chinese, especially during the Sino-Japanese war (1937–45). During the First World War when the European nations were otherwise preoccupied, she had taken over bases in French Indo-China, forced the closure of the Burma Road by Britain and drew up plans against the oil-and rubber-rich British, American and Dutch possessions and bases to the south.

On the Allied side, the defence of the vast Far Eastern area against an attack by Japan had been the subject of speculation and planning for twenty years before the Second World War. But no convincing air defence had resulted. For a start, each nation worked out its own defence plan for its own territory. Liaison was rare. Both the principal British and American plans rested on their superior sea-power. Each individually had plans to provoke a major surface naval battle based on variations of the 1916 Battle of Jutland when the battleships of each side were supposed to decide the issue. Air power was very much peripheral to such a set-piece concept.

Prior to the outbreak of the war the British had not been entirely blind to the options open to the Japanese in this part of the world. A meeting of the British Combined Chiefs of Staff (Admiral of the Fleet Sir Dudley Pound, General Sir John Dill, and Air Chief Marshal Sir Cyril Newall) in August 1941, drew up a scenario of just such a series of moves by the Japanese. They admitted at the outset that, in the many previous assessments on this subject, the move of a main British battle fleet to the Far East had always been taken for granted. This now proved impossible because of losses and commitments in home waters, the Arctic and the Mediterranean. Neither had any pre-war British assessment ever taken into consideration a situation in which the Japanese had virtually overrun South China, and both French Indo-China and Thailand had become potential bases for the Japanese air forces; but this was the case that faced them in December 1941. Nor did they ever seriously consider the necessity of defending British Borneo. In addition, that the main American Pacific Fleet might be knocked out right at the start of the war and thus be unable to intervene at all was not even contemplated, let alone studied, in August 1941.

The main British concern at this time was to defend Malaya and the Dutch East Indies. In the event they had neither enough aircraft nor a sufficient battle fleet to provide either a deterrent or a bar. However, in the south-west Pacific area the

Chiefs of Staff considered that the trans-Pacific trade routes were important in connection with supplies from America to Australasia and the Far East (which was prophetic enough), as well as providing an alternative channel of communication with the United Kingdom if difficulties should arise on the Cape route. Their summing-up is highly pertinent to how things eventually turned out: 'The distances from Japan are considerable, but there would be nothing to prevent the Japanese Government (provided they were not deterred by fear of American action) establishing advanced fuelling bases in the South Sea Islands in order to facilitate operations in the south-west Pacific.'

The Chiefs of Staff added that, should such a course of action commend itself to Japan then there were 'innumerable potential bases in these island which could not all be defended from Japanese attack'. One final piece of advice was added: 'From the Japanese point of view it would clearly be preferable to seize a harbour with existing base facilities, particularly Suva in Fiji.'

However, having, in August 1941, spelled out the Japanese threat almost exactly as it actually took place a few months later, the Chiefs of Staff undid their foresight by stating that, in their opinion, 'no serious threat to the territorial integrity of Australia and New Zealand would be likely to arise at least until Japan had consolidated her position in China and the Far East, *which would take a considerable time.*' Alas, it did not.

On the British side, by 1941 the involvement of the bulk of her armed forces against the combined threats of Germany and Italy in Europe, the Mediterranean and the Atlantic tied down all but a fraction of available forces. What equipment could be spared was in the main obsolete or second-rate, understandably the best aircraft were kept back in the crucial combat zones. Others were shipped to Russia. The defence of the British Far Eastern possessions – to the anxiety of Australia, New Zealand, Malaya and, to a lesser extent, India – were left with a few fighter squadrons equipped with Brewster Buffalo and Hawker Hurricane fighters, while offensive air power lay with totally obsolete Wildebeeste torpedo-bombers and the like, and very few of those. Plans were made to fly some Blenheim twin-engined bombers from the Middle East, but these carried small bomb loads and were of the standard level-bombing types which rarely achieved destructive hits.

The American Army Air Force had not developed dive-bombers at all until the German Stuka victories in Europe. Then General 'Hap' Arnold ordered the formation of such units and the development of new dive-bombing aircraft. Plans were laid for large numbers of Brewster Buccaneers, Curtiss Shrikes and Vultee Vengeances to be built, but these were long-term projects. In the short-term all the USAAF could do was form squadrons equipped with converted Douglas Dauntless dive-bombers, termed the A–24, and ship those hastily to the battle zone.

It was one thing to equip units, however, quite another to make up for twenty years' neglect in operating techniques. Dive-bombing requires both natural skill and application. The theory can be learnt, the skills can be practised, but there was little time to do either in the first few months of the Far Eastern war.

The other Allies were equally as unprepared. Australia quickly converted some of her single-engined Wirraway fighters to carry light bombs under their wings and used them in action; the Dutch defenders of Sumatra and Java had little in the way of air power to halt the invaders. Improvisation was the order of the day. In the main this policy failed to stem the onrush of Japanese expansion in the Far East. Only in one outstanding example did it pay off.

When the Pacific War broke out, in December 1941, it was the Japanese and American navies which still possessed the only great fleets of dive-bombers in the Pacific area, all other air arms there had still resolutely set their faces against it, despite the lessons of Europe. Thus it was the dive-bombers of the Imperial Japanese Navy which spearheaded Japan's breathtaking advances in the early months. They dropped the first bombs on Pearl Harbor on 7 December 1941. They led the attacks against the American forces in the Philippines. They decimated Port Darwin in Australia. They smashed the British Indian Ocean squadron of Sir James Somerville in April 1942

when the aircraft carrier *Hermes* and the cruisers *Dorsetshire*
and *Cornwall* were sunk. They traded blows with the American
Dauntless dive-bombers at the Battle of the Coral Sea in May
1942.

But these were almost all carrier-based operations. Flying
from the decks of these great ships the Aichi 'Val' dive-bombers
demolished the enemy with clinical precision. Then, finally,
when they confronted American dive-bombers at the Battle of
Midway in June 1942, all those priceless aircraft and their
highly skilled aircrew were lost in one devastating attack. The
Japanese navy's dive-bomber arm never fully recovered from
this massive blow.

But they had already established a whole new empire within a
few months. Now that empire needed to be defended. It was, in
the main, a jungle-clad empire: from the northern and western
boundaries of British Burma, where it touched India and
China, in a wide sweep through Malaya, the Dutch East Indies
(Sumatra, Java and Timor), across New Britain and New
Ireland and the northern fringes of New Guinea, and down to
the island chain of the Solomons to Tulagi and Guadalcanal.
The whole sweep of tangled jungle and dense rain forest, of
uncharted hills and impenetrable islands, this forgotten corner of the world, now became the very crucible of the dive-
bomber war. Initially the Japanese Naval Air Corps, formed
and equipped with the Aichi D–3A dive-bomber which the
Allies had code-named 'Val', consisted of 31 N A C, formed on 1
February 1942 in the Philippines and initially used especially in
supporting the army's operations at Bataan and Corregidor; 33
N A C, formed at Saeki, Japan at the same time, and at first
based at Makasar in the Celebes from 2 March 1942, in order
similarly to support the invasion and occupation of Java and
other islands in the Dutch East Indies; and 35 N A C, with
another 12 Vals, also utilised in that area.

The occupation of the Dutch East Indies by the Japanese
followed the fall of Borneo and Malaya but took place while
fighting was still going on in the last Allied strongholds in the
Philippines and Singapore. The outcome of these audacious
invasions had already been largely decided by several vicious

sea battles which had resulted in the annihilation of Allied sea power in the area. Although they had no dive-bombers themselves the Dutch defenders tried using Brewster 339 fighter aircraft in such a role on 23 January 1942 with small 110-lb bombs under their wings. Again they attacked a Japanese convoy in the Makasar Strait but failed to inflict any damage on the Japanese vessels.

These operations also saw the limited use of US land-based dive-bomber units but only for a brief period. 27 Bombardment Group was equipped with the A–24, which the US Army Air Force had named the Banshee, and sailed for the Philippines as early as November 1941. Long before they could arrive the deteriorating situation led to the planes being re-routed to Brisbane in Australia where they were unloaded and used to equip 91 Bombardment Squadron.

This unit moved into the Dutch East Indies in time to take part in the defence of those islands but achieved nothing. It partook only of one operational sortie, an attack on the Japanese invasion fleet off Java on 29 February 1942. Seven Banshees claimed two hits on a enemy cruiser, but in fact had failed to score any, and they lost two of their number in the attack. The surviving aircraft were immediately pulled out of the island and sent back to Australia.

During the final days of the Philippines campaign the four surviving P–40 fighters remaining to the US Army Air Force were fitted with 500-lb bombs and pressed into service as dive-bombers. They attacked Japanese transports in Subic Bay and claimed to have sunk one on 2 March, but they lost one P–40 and the other three were so badly damaged that they were written off. However, the relative success of this adaptation had significant impact elsewhere in the embattled eastern theatre.

Another American A–24 unit was the 8 Bombardment Squadron which remained based in northern Australia. It also operated in vain against the Japanese invaders. When the Japanese established airfields at Lae and Salamaua the Banshees made attacks accompanied by RAAF Kittyhawk fighters in the strafing role but, on 29 July, an A–24 mission by seven dive-bombers against Japanese positions on Buna Island ended in disaster. Zero fighters intercepted them and destroyed all save one of the American machines. This shook to the core the already uncertain faith of the Air Corps in dive-bombers.

The southern Pacific at that date had marked the high-water mark of Japanese expansion to cut off Australia from her sole source of outside help, the United States. Here twin drives, south to Port Moresby on the south-western coast of New Guinea, and down the Solomon Islands chain towards Fiji, were continuing, despite the setback in the central Pacific.

Far away along the blazing arc that was spreading across the area lay Burma. Here a small Japanese army, used to living off the land and moving through jungle terrain, had struck and sent the limited Allied forces reeling back on yet another front. No dive-bombers were available to either side during the first weeks of the 'longest retreat in the history of the British Army'. Both air forces used medium bombers, on the British side mostly Blenheims, on the Japanese side Kawasaki Ki48s. In one attack on 21 March at Lashio almost the whole remaining Allied air force was wiped out on the ground.

Opposing the Kawasakis had been Hawker Hurricanes of the RAF and P–40 fighters of the American Volunteer Group (AVG), the 'Flying Tigers'. Pre-war reaction to Japan's continual aggression had led to the reopening of the Burma Road, the resupply of the Chinese Nationalist Army of Chiang Kai-shek and the oil embargo against her. But even before these political moves had reached fruition a group of volunteer fighter pilots under an American Army Air Officer named Clair Lee Chennault had recruited a mercenary force to aid the Chinese in their desperate resistance. Partly through idealistic concepts, partly through financial reward, experienced military pilots from the United States Navy, Marine Corps and Army Air Corps were recruited and sent to form a hard-fighting unit long before America herself became involved in the war. Recruitment of these volunteers from existing service units was given the 'blind eye' treatment by many in authority at the time and even their voyage across the Pacific to Burma was given 'unofficial' warship escort by the Americans and the Dutch navies while the British made an old RAF base at Toungoo available to them when they formed up and trained.

Supply of suitable aircraft was, however, another problem.

The terms and conditions of the American Volunteer Group laid down that they were to be strictly a defensive unit, a fighter unit to protect the defenceless Chinese towns and cities from the continual and almost unopposed daylight bombing of the Japanese army and navy long-range bombers. Chennault had, however, to get what pilots he could and this included many ex-bomber pilots. At first, given their determined role, this was something of a handicap and teaching bomber pilots how to fly fighters slowed down the time required to get the unit into shape for combat. Some took to their new calling easily and absorbed the new lessons quickly. For example both Bob Neale and David 'Tex' Hill were ex-navy dive-bomber pilots. In subsequent fighter interception roles they had among the best combat records of the entire group. But their old talents and skills were soon to pay an unexpected but handsome, dividend.

The P–40 (the P stood for Pursuit) Warhawk, and its later Kittyhawk derivative, was itself a sturdy but unremarkable single-seater, low-wing, monoplane, powered by a single Allison 1200-hp in-line engine. First developed in 1938 and ordered by the US Army in April 1939 it was a contemporary of the Hawker Hurricane and Messerschmitt Bf109 but inferior to both.

Perhaps the P–40's most distinctive feature was the coolant radiator associated with an oil cooler in a combined cowling under the aircraft's nose. Number 112 Squadron RAF, using this mount in the Middle East, painted a shark's mouth and teeth over this feature, markings that were subsequently copied by many other nations and gave it a visual trademark that became famous. The 'Flying Tigers' of Chennault's conception were no exceptions but they also used to change the colour of the prop spinner from red to blue to yellow to green frequently to try and mislead the Japanese as to their true, pitifully small, numbers.

By April 1942, with the fall of Lashio, the fate of Burma was settled. The British were pulling back into Assam, along with the forces of the American General 'Vinegar Joe' Stilwell, who was President Roosevelt's military representative to Chiang-Kai-shek, and Chief of Staff and Military Adviser to the

Chinese government. Chennault had pulled his fighters back to Kunming, their old base in Yunnan province, now threatened on every side by Japanese forces for what looked like the last stand. The Burma Road was no longer a vital supply link for the Chinese armies but an open high road for the Japanese invaders to pour north across the Chinese frontier in an increasing flood, using the ample motor transports provided by the fleeing Allied armies and spearheaded by their crack Red Dragon Armoured Division. There seemed little left to stop them.

The Chinese had very few bomber aircraft, a squadron of obsolete Russian SBs and one of their equally obsolete Curtiss Hawk biplane dive-bombers was the most they could spare. Repeated demands by Chennault to the States for his own bomber force fell on deaf ears. He was not popular among his own contemporaries in the Army Air Corps (which became the US Army Air Force in 1942) because long ago he had disdainfully dismissed their obsession with the heavy bomber concept as illogical.

Despite the fact that, from his own experience in China before the war, he knew more about the Japanese aircraft and methods of aerial combat than any other Allied air commander, they were also dismissive of his other theories. Content to let his 'mercenaries' do the fighting while they built up their strength far away in India in pursuit of long-term strategic concepts, they could not grasp that the situation in spring 1942 called for immediate action if China was to be kept in the war at all. They were consistent in their efforts to have this 'rebel' unit incorporated back under the Army Air Corps command again so they could control it, and the date of 1 July 1942 was decided upon. But events meanwhile were pressing. Japanese troops had taken the border town of Wanting on 3 May and crossed into Yunnan. Only the upper reaches of the Salween and Mekong rivers stood between them and Kunming.

With the Japanese column already in China and fast approaching the west rim of the Salween gorge there were still thousands of Chinese civilian refugees and soldiers straggling up the road west of the Salween. Allied pilots reported that Japanese motorised columns were moving up the centre of the road between these swarms of unarmed Chinese soldiers and civilians. Should the Japanese make their way unopposed it was only a matter of time before they would penetrate to Kunming itself. Should this city fall it could easily mean the end of the war for China as well, for the Japanese would then control the only practical supply route to China. Access via the deserts of Turkestan and Mongolia from Russia was ruled out, for the Soviet Union at the time was fighting for her very life against the German onslaught on the European Front. As Chennault wrote later:

> I was faced with one of those grim decisions that come to every military man so often in battle issuing orders that meant the sacrifice of a few to save the many. We had small stomach for bombing and machine-gunning those refugees on the west bank of the Salween, but if we were going to stop the Japs, we would have to slaughter some innocents along the road. I radioed Madame Chiang in Chungking on 6 May.

Madame Chiang answered: 'Generalissimo instructs you send all available A V G to attack trucks, boats etc between Salween and Lungling city.'

So Chennault had his orders, but how to comply with them with only a few fighter aircraft? Already attempts had been made to adapt the P–40B for bombing with home-made bomb racks, but these had proven abortive. They had tried everything, 'including dropping whisky bottles filled with gasoline as incendiaries and pushing lead-pipe bombs through the flare chutes'. Chennault himself spent long hours at the machine shop at Kunming trying to cobble together an external bomb rack that would function on the P–40B, but in vain. In the opinion of some of his flyers the whole concept was a crazy one anyway. Ex-Marine flyer Boyington wrote scathingly:

> Some of our fast-diving P–40s were being converted into dive-bombers. A dive-bomber should not pick up too much speed in a dive, therefore the engineers design dive brakes into them to slow them down while diving. But not here. They loaded the bombs on a ship that picked up speed in a dive faster than any other that existed at the time, and started dive-bombing, resulting in more pilots lost. I'd had sufficient dive-bombing experience to know that these converted bombers didn't even have to be shot down. This was the final straw.

It was not until the arrival of the Model Es that the difficulties were overcome. The P–40E was a re-design of the original Hawk 81A with a 1150-hp Allison engine, six wing-mounted guns, and a built-in hardpoint under the fuselage for carrying either a 52 US-gallon drop-tank for range or a 500-lb bomb. This was the Kittyhawk. As before, Chennault had the greatest difficulty laying his hands on a few of these aircraft, but eventually, just in time, he was able to do so.

The US 10 Air Force was being assembled in India by Major-General Lewis H. Brereton. He had seen defeat in the Philippines and Dutch East Indies and wished to avoid a third humiliation for American arms by building up a powerful force before letting it loose on the enemy rather than make piecemeal efforts. When the new P–40Es were ferried in via Takoradi in West Africa for the AVG, who had bought them for cash in the United States, he held on to them for his command. Even though the Chinese had also already paid cash for these planes it took a direct protest by Chiang Kai-shek to President Roosevelt before Brereton was persuaded to release the urgently required P–40Es to the American Volunteer Group.

As well as the hard-pad beneath the fuselage the P–40E was equipped with wing bomb racks. Two of the AVG's armourers modified the underbelly bomb rack so that it could carry a single 570-lb Russian high-explosive bomb, of which there were enormous stocks left in unoccupied China.

Some of the former Volunteer Group pilots were ex-navy dive-bombers from the carrier *Yorktown*. They could now put into practice their hard-learned skills against the Japanese, and if not a Japanese aircraft-carrier, then an enemy target of equal and vital importance. Eight pilots all volunteered for the first dive-bombing missions.

By noon on 6 May it was reported that the advance guard of the Japanese armoured column, including artillery and truck-loads of infantry, had reached the west bank of the river Salween. The suspension bridge had been blown up by the retreating Chinese but this did not halt their advance for long for an engineering unit was on its way to throw a pontoon bridge across the Salween. Meanwhile the Japanese advance came to a temporary halt at the river's edge while their trucks, armoured cars and cannon built up to present a tempting and vulnerable target as they spread all down the twenty miles of road on the western escarpment leading to the crossing. The area was to the east of Wanting where the Salween crosses the border in a deep river-gorge carved out of the rock. The Burma Road, on which the enemy column lay exposed, was hewn out of the jungle ridges along the edge of this great gash, winding its way down its precipitous edges like a coiled snake, with hairpin bends and knife-edge drops until the bridge is reached. Having taken Kutki, and with firm supply lines up from Lashio, the enemy was determined to cut this remaining corridor between China and its retreating allies. On 4 May a massive air strike by fifty Japanese bombers was made against Paoshan and many refugees became casualties, adding to the panic of the retreat. The Chinese seemed demoralised and about to disintegrate.

The dive-bombers were ready by 6 May. Now was the only time left for the AVG's young dive-bomber pilots to strike a decisive blow. Although the headquarters and the bulk of his slender forces were held at Kunming, Chennault had another small section of the American Volunteer Group located, prior to the Japanese aerial attack, at Paoshan. Five P-40s had been based there in order to protect AVG supply routes from Burma, while at Yunnanyi, a point midway between Paoshan and Kunming, a third section, comprising a radio and servicing detachment, had been set up. This was also to serve as a refuelling and emergency landing field. During the Paoshan attack on 4 May only one AVG fighter, piloted by Charlie Bond from Dallas, Texas, got up in time to intercept and he shot down two bombers. Another pilot, Ben C. Foshee of Red Level, Alabama, was killed by the bombing while trying to reach his plane. On 5 May, however, the AVG hit back when nine P-40s intercepted a further Japanese bomber group and claimed to have destroyed eight. It was while these desperate defensive struggles were taking place that returning P-40 reconnaissance planes revealed the dire situation on the Burma Road.

Chennault's wife later wrote how, that same evening,

he held a blackboard council of war with his pilots. The AVG armourers, Roy Hoffman of Athens, Ohio, and Charlie Baisden of Scranton, Pennsylvania, rigged bomb racks for 570-lb bombs under the bellies of four Kittyhawk P–40Es and loaded the wing racks with fragmentation bombs. For weeks Chennault had been pleading with Washington for light bombers with which he would be able to attack the mechanized Japanese columns driving up from Burma; but the improvised bomb racks on the P–40Es was the best he could do at the moment. Previous experiments to mount makeshift racks for the old P–40Bs had not been successful.

Logic dictated the composition of the striking force. Four of the most experienced dive-bomber pilots were chosen to fly the converted Kittyhawks. The leader was David 'Tex' Hill. He was accompanied by Tom Jones, Ed Rector and Frank Lawlor, all former US Navy dive-bomber pilots. Others who volunteered for the Salween gorge bombing mission included Lou Bishop, Lind (C. H.) Laughlin, Jr., Frank Schiel, and Bob Little.

To provide limited air cover and back up with strafing support, three ex-Army Corps fighter pilots were picked to fly unconverted P–40Bs. These were Arvid S. Olson, as flight commander, with R. T. 'Tadpole' Smith and Erik Shilling, a trio of ex-Army pilots, along with Tom Hayward, formerly of the Marine Corps. All arms of the United States forces were thus represented.

The eight-plane force was ready for its historic mission by dawn on 7 May. The dive-bombers and their escorts took off in the dim half-light and formed up over the field before heading off due west towards the enemy. The P–40Es had fragmentation bombs on their wing racks in addition to the main bomb under the fuselage.

They cleared the Mekong between Tali and Chenyuan after encountering weather conditions that threatened to abort the mission before it started. The long-heralded monsoon season was approaching and the distant rumbles of what were soon to develop into torrential downpours and bring low-cloud ceilings were beginning to be felt. Most campaigning stopped for, in the monsoon season, flying became near impossible, and conditions on the ground even more appalling than normal. If the enemy could be held back now there would be time to re-group and re-form, and vital breathing space would be won.

Over Paoshan, on the very edge of the Shan hills guarding the deep cleft of the Salween, the Flying Tigers encountered this bad weather. Like a black wall, toweringly tall thunderheads blocked their route. The tactical situation on the ground, however, allowed for little hesitation on the part of Tex Hill. After circling for a while to weigh up the situation he led his little squadron resolutely onwards. Straight ahead they plunged right into the storm, hoping that clearer weather might prevail over the target area. Fortune favoured the brave on this occasion for, after a turbulent quarter-of-an-hour of blind flying, they came out of the storm into the bright sunlight and there, ahead of them, was the gorge flanked by the Kao Li Kung mountains. In fact the rainstorm was a blessing in disguise for it had cleared the dusty atmosphere at just the right moment and opened up a crystal-clear panorama. As Chennault's wife later recorded:

> The sight that met the eyes of the eager Tiger pilots was almost too good to be true. Ahead, and etched against the towering rock cliffs of the steep, twenty-mile winding descent to the muddy Salween at the bottom of the knifelike gorge, was the entire Japanese military force. Japanese engineers were working frantically to unload pontoons out of trucks and into the river. Miraculously, there was no sign of Japanese air support. Evidently the Japanese high command believed that the American Volunteer Group had been pounded out of existence.

The entire enemy column of tanks, trucks, guns and soldiers – along, alas, with streams of refugees – lay open and trapped, with a sheer rock face one side of them and the deep gorge on the other. There was little place for them to hide as they were clear of the all-embracing jungle behind them.

The dive-bombers' first target was the topmost edges of the rock wall itself, in order to start landslides and block the retreat of the main force. Waggling his aircraft wings Tex Hill led the four bombers down in a diving attack – not a truly vertical attack since the Kittyhawk could not take the strains of this but at an angle of about 70 degrees.

Resistance from the ground was slight. The Japanese were caught completely by surprise and the four big bombs exploded exactly on target, bringing down great slippages of earth and rocks and trapping the rear of the enemy column against the rocky escarpment:

> Huge boulders, landslides of rubble, trucks, ammunition and human bodies exploded in a shattering blast that piled up into a bloody barricade barring any possible retreat for the Japanese [continued Chennault's wife's account]. Pulling out of their dive, the Kittyhawks climbed steeply, dipped their needle-like noses, and came screaming in again, this time with all of their fifty-calibre machine guns spewing deadly lead. Simultaneously, they unleashed the fragmentation bombs under the Kittyhawks' wings which tore great holes in the truck and infantry columns, already faltering to a halt because of the sudden incredible attack which had literally come out of the blue.

With the column demoralised the Kittyhawks shuttled back and forth strafing with their wing machine-guns to add to the havoc until they had emptied all their ammunition. There was still no sign of enemy fighter cover and so Tex called down his own umbrella to take over what his dive-bombers had started. The four fighters carried out numerous sweeps against the pontoon equipment itself to render it, and the engineers, unusable.

Not a single P–40 was hit in return and all eight returned to Kunming unharmed. Here they were quickly refuelled and rearmed with fragmentation bombs and incendiaries. A second strike was away within a short period, this time led by Jim Howard. Again they encountered no aerial opposition and, although light flak was more evident, there were again no losses. The second wave contributed more misery and devastation to the hitherto invincible Japanese tank crews for whom there was no cover, and left behind them a huge column of black smoke over the Salween gorge to mark the graveyard of the crack enemy columns.

Nor was this to be the end of their misery. For four successive days Chennault threw his small force into attack after attack to complete the rout. The Chinese SB–3 bombers also made one attack but were in such a poor condition that, although all returned, they were never able to take off again. The Chinese also threw in their Hawk dive-bombers and these, combined with the Kittyhawks, made repeated attacks on the broken column as it made its painful way back to the Burmese border.

Encouraged by this brilliant success the Chinese army rallied. In order to stop the rot the Japanese threw in a second armoured division to escort more motorised troops up from Lashio, but it met the same fate as the first when it was caught by the Kittyhawks led by Frank Schiel just below Lungling. Again precision dive-bombing, followed by wholesale strafing, won the day and sent the enemy reeling back in disorder a second time.

A whole supply column of petrol tankers was also decimated; some fifty tankers, it was claimed, had been left burning after one attack. Even if the Japanese had the will to make a third try this deprived them of the means to keep their tanks and lorries moving in sufficient numbers to win through. By 11 May the advance of the Japanese army had been stopped cold. The remnants of the Red Dragon Division were stumbling back thankfully towards the distant sanctuary of Lungling. The next day Chennault was able to send this second signal to Madame Chiang Kai-shek:

> AVG flight bombed and machine-gunned 75–100 Jap trucks headed south yesterday. Rear of column just entering Wanting City while head was south of city. More than twenty trucks burned, many more damaged. Return fire from light tanks in column. Reconnaissance along road back to Salween discovered only single trucks at long intervals. Believe no Jap unit large as battalion now north of Wanting. Reconnaissance this morning along west bank Salween discovered no sign of Japs.

Further attacks were made by the AVG until mid-May when the monsoon finally closed down the campaigning season, but by then the crisis had passed and the front line here settled down to a two-year stalemate. The attack on the Salween gorge in fact marked the high tide of Japanese penetration of China from the south-west. It was also a decisive victory, a victory, moreover, which influenced the whole future course of the Asian war. Yet outside America it is hardly known.

More than anything else it was a victory achieved by dive-bombing. Once again, as at Sedan in France in 1940, in Crete in 1941 and at Tobruk in 1942, as well as at Pearl Harbor and Midway in the Pacific, and in a whole host of other actions, the value of a few precision attacks had been amply demonstrated.

3
Rabaul and Guadalcanal

By the summer of 1942 the first targets of the grandiose Japanese plan to conquer South-East Asia had been completed; moreover, they had been completed ahead of schedule and with an extremely low casualty rate. In addition the defeats which the Japanese had inflicted upon the Allied forces: the sinking of the main US battleship force at Pearl Harbor; the sinking of the British capital ships *Prince of Wales* and *Repulse* off Malaya; the naval victories of the Java Sea and the Indian Ocean; and the easy conquests of Burma, Malaya, Singapore, Borneo, the Philippines and the Dutch East Indies, were unexpectedly severe and far-reaching. In many of these victories, too, precision power, accurately applied by carrier-based dive-bombers, had played a notable part.

But the temptation to go further was irresistible and, from the summer of 1942, the Japanese ran into increasingly fierce resistance. Their headlong rush was first halted, then held, and painfully and slowly reversed. The first indecisive naval battle, that of the Coral Sea in May 1942, was followed by an overwhelming defeat at Midway in June 1942. Despite this Japanese plans for yet further expansion – southward towards Port Moresby to threaten Australia, south-eastward towards Samoa, and westward into the Indian plain – continued but, even so, on the various fronts at their tropical extremes the land fighting began to stagnate. Instead of continual withdrawal, the Allies made stands and hard fighting began to predominate. It was a change forced upon the Japanese, from victorious pursuit to stubborn defence, because of the application by the Allies of dive-bombing on a large scale.

In the re-organisation of the Japanese Naval Air Service squadrons in the aftermath of the disastrous Midway battle – when the cream of their carrier-borne dive-bomber crews had

been wiped out without being given a chance to contribute to
the outcome – it was clear that a greater reliance would have to
be placed on land-based dive-bombers, to hold the island 'ring'
until the fleet could be re-constructed and equipped with the
new Naval Air Corps and their Aichi D–3A dive-bombers.

March 1942 marked the high-water mark of Japanese expansion into the southern Pacific which aimed to cut Australia off
from the United States. Japan's twin drives, however, to Port
Moresby on the south-western coast of New Guinea, and down
the Solomon Islands chain towards Fiji, were continuing.
Although the easier seaborne landings against Port Moresby
had been forestalled by the battle of the Coral Sea, in their place
an overland drive was being made across the mountains of the
Owen Stanley range. In the other direction the advance down
the island chain of the Solomon Group had reached the small
island of Tulagi, where a main base was being established,
while on the much larger island of Guadalcanal a supporting
airstrip was being hacked out of the jungle in readiness for the
next step forward. All these moves were supplied and supported from the hub of Japanese power in that part of the
Pacific, Rabaul, on the north-western tip of New Britain.

Rabaul had been the seat of government for the pre-war
Australian administration, but its defences were meagre. A few
months before outbreak of hostilities the civilian airfield at
Lakunai had been converted into a fighter strip, and Army
engineers were building a bomber strip at Vunakanua. The first
RAAF aircraft to arrive there, in October 1941, had been
Hudson heavy bombers and Wirraway fighters but the Hud-
sons were forced to withdraw following Japanese air raids in
December 1941 and January 1942, and the Japanese 17 Army
had assembled a 4000-strong force at Truk in the Carolines in
readiness to invade.

This invasion took place during the night of 22–23 January
against the western shore of Karavia Bay and Simpson Harbour, and the town fell on the same day. Close air support for
the Japanese was provided by a hundred fighters and dive-
bombers which faced no aerial opposition and an anti-aircraft
defence which comprised two 3-in. HA-guns. By midday these

navy dive-bombers were operating from Lakunai airfield despite attempts by the retreating Australians to mine it. Subsequent landings took place at New Ireland and Duke of York islands where garrisons were established. On 9 February Gasmata in New Britain and the Papuan Peninsula were invaded, followed a month later by the occupation of Lae and Salamaua.

The Japanese navy landed next at Buka Island on 13 March and began to build an airstrip, and further beachheads were quickly established at Buin on Bougainville and, in late May, further down the Solomon chain on Guadalcanal itself where another airstrip was begun. However, it was not until August that this airfield, destined to play such a significant role in the war in the Pacific, was nearing completion.

Meanwhile Rabaul itself was being developed and strengthened into the major Japanese base and staging post for their twin drives south and south-west. By June 1942 25 and 26 Air Flotillas were based there along with the 958 and Yokohama Groups, but at this time they did not have dive-bombers on their strength: navy units flew in and out as required. On the very day that Headquarters in Rabaul planned to fly the first aircraft into Guadalcanal, the US Marines effected a landing there and the struggle for the Solomon Islands began in earnest.

Rabaul town itself, standing on the northern shore of the superb Simpson Harbour, provided a good protected anchorage off Blanche Bay which was further flanked by Matupi Island. Across the top of the Gazelle Peninsula the Japanese soon constructed a series of airfields, storage dumps, army and navy command posts, and coastal and anti-aircraft batteries until the tip of New Britain became a bastion from which the tentacles of the Japanese octopus radiated across the whole region.

One of the pilots based there from the earliest days described his initial reaction to Rabaul:

> I could not believe what I saw. If Bali had been a paradise, then Rabaul was plucked from the very depths of hell itself. There was a narrow and dusty airstrip which was to serve our group. It was the worst airfield I had ever seen anywhere. Immediately behind this wretched runway a ghastly volcano loomed 700ft into the air.

Every few minutes the ground trembled and the volcano groaned deeply, then hurled out stones and thick, choking smoke. Behind the volcano stood pallid mountains stripped of all their trees and foliage.

To these early airstrips others were soon added so that eventually there were five. One was built close to Rabaul town itself, across the Sulphur Creek at Lakunai; another was located to the south-west at Keravat, on the neck of the largest peninsula, Vunakanua. Off Lesson Point to the east was Raporo, while yet another strip was located further south between these two, at Tobera. All these airfields were soon well stocked with army but mainly navy aircraft and presented a bristling hedgehog of attack and defence. As time went on underground bunkers and command posts, as well as ammunition dumps and food stores, were hacked out of the ground to escape the endless bombing by the Allies.

Initially the main occupants of these airfields were the aircraft of 25 Air Flotilla under the overall command of Rear-Admiral Sadayoshi Yamada, and its medium bombers were able to attack targets in New Guinea and elsewhere under the protection of Zero fighter escorts. However, the standard routine of Rabaul base changed for ever when, on 7 August 1942, the United States Marines waded ashore at Tulagi and also took the airstrip on Guadalcanal itself, which they renamed Henderson Field. Around this jungle-clad, malaria-ridden island and this solitary airstrip was waged one of the fiercest land, sea and air campaigns of the whole war. For months the Japanese tried to wrest back the lost airfield while the Americans grimly clung on to it. Pitched battles were fought ashore and in the waters leading down between the islands which became known as 'The Slot'. In the air also it became the main battleground, a dogged slugging match between the two sides.

In this battle the flight distances involved from Rabaul to the battle-zone became the crucial element. The one-way flight was 550 nautical miles, beyond the 874 miles' overall range of the 'Val' dive-bombers which the Japanese navy had rushed into Rabaul as part of their initial response to the American landings. In their book *Zero!*, Masatake Okumiyra and Jiro Horikoshi recalled: 'Our "Val" dive-bombers, however, were dispatched in missions on which their crews despaired of survival. Simply stated, the aircraft could not carry sufficient fuel to make the round-trip flight from Rabaul to Guadalcanal and return.'

Many of the eighteen Aichis that failed to return during the first two days of the attacks were lost for this reason alone. Japanese construction teams were quickly set to work to hack out new, intermediate bases on intervening islands, the first at Buka on Bougainville Island, which was occupied during the night of 12–13 August, but this was not occupied until 27 August. For the first weeks' operations, the situation in the southern Solomons was so desperate that the dive-bombers were sent into the attack anyway, almost suicide missions in fact.

As soon as news came in of the landings, a force of 27 'Betty' medium bombers, armed with bombs instead of the more normal and more effective torpedoes, was dispatched by 25 Air Flotilla, along with an escort of Zero fighters. A second attack was sent in the same afternoon, consisting of 16 'Val' dive-bombers. Both waves were intercepted by American Wildcat fighters from the aircraft carriers *Enterprise, Saratoga* and *Wasp*. A VF6 Combat Air Patrol (CAP) of four Grumman F–4F fighters, led by Lieutenant A. O. Vorse, was protecting the fleet at the time. At 14.00, when radar sighting of the incoming attack was made, an additional six Wildcats were scrambled away to assist in repelling the assault.

The first visual sighting was made by Vorse at 14.30 over Savo Island. He spotted three incoming 'Vals' making their approach towards the transport anchorage at Tulagi from the south, the direction of Guadalcanal.

The Japanese dive-bombers, when first seen, were at the same altitude as the fighters, but it was clear that they would soon begin their attack dives on the ships. There was no time for finesse, and so VF6 charged straight in towards the port side of the 'V' formation and opened fire on the rearmost Aichi at long range. Forewarned by this the dive-bomber tipped over his nose into the dive in the hope of throwing the Wildcats off target and at the same time getting in his bombing run. The usual dive-bomber tactic at this stage was to open the dive-brakes, thus slowing the aircraft down and causing the pursuing fighter to overshoot. Vorse was prepared for this tactic but it did not occur. This proved fatal for the Japanese pilot as Vorse was able to continue to pour in concentrated fire on the 'Val'. He broke off his attack at 2000ft and observed the dive-bomber crash into the sea almost centrally in 'The Slot' between the islands. However, the other American fighters were not so fortunate and, when the other 'Vals' tipped over into their attacks, the fighters 'lost' them almost immediately.

Meanwhile the reinforcing F–4Fs had been warned over the radio that the attack was imminent, but it was the sight of black shell-bursts as the leading 'Vals' began their dives that first revealed the enemy had arrived. Lieutenant Daniel Runyon assumed that the logical object of their attentions were the Marine transports and he led his unit directly to the landing beaches at Red One, Guadalcanal. He and Lieutenant Packard at once sighted a solitary Aichi over Lunga Point and made a concerted attack on it. Unsupported, and with two fighters on his tail, the unfortunate Japanese airman stood little chance. Under Packard's fire the 'Val' exploded in mid-air, the debris raining down into Ironbottom Sound.

Almost at once after the two Wildcats happened on their first victims – a Wingman, having also become separated, was heading alone straight towards the American fighters. Caught in a cone of fire from both, the dive-bomber was soon dispatched. On completion of this pass Runyon saw two more dive-bombers which had completed their attacks and were making their get-away low over the water to the north-west. At 500ft Runyon dispatched one of these while Lieutenants March and Shoemaker concentrated on the other, which they also destroyed.

This first dive-bomber assault had proven a massacre, all but two of the 'Vals' being claimed as shot down. Their only recorded success was a hit on the destroyer *Mugford* which only damaged her slightly.

Next day the 'Betty' bombers were sent back with torpedoes

and 26 of them bravely pressed in their attacks at very low level on the anchored invasion fleet; but the Americans were prepared and shot down 17 of them. Again a follow-up attack was launched with many 'Vals' again shot down. Two dive-bombers, which had been heavily hit by anti-aircraft fire, chose not to pull out of their dives but aimed instead at the American ships. One of them, further and repeatedly hit, blew up in mid-air but the other crashed on to the American troop transport *George F. Elliott* which caught fire and burned all night before she sank; but this was their sole success. However, the three American aircraft-carriers were prematurely withdrawn that same day leaving the Marines without air support.

Admiral Isoroku Yamamoto was disturbed that the Americans had established themselves firmly ashore. He warned Admiral Mikawa:

> The situation at Guadalcanal is very serious, more serious than that which faced our fathers when they understood that they had to occupy Port Arthur before the arrival of the Baltic Fleet. If we do not act at once with three more divisions we must expect very grave consequences.

He was to be proved correct, but even Yamamoto could not foresee the bitterness, the scale and the duration of the struggle for the Solomon Islands, nor how it was ultimately to decimate all of Japan's forces in the area. A war of attrition was the very type of war Japan could not afford to fight whereas America, with her vast resources of material, manpower and money, could. Nor could anyone have foreseen how it was to lead to Yamamoto's own sudden death.

Having expended almost all their immediately available air strength to no avail, the Japanese had to draw up new plans. Reinforcements were drafted into Rabaul in readiness for an offensive in August to drive the invader from Guadalcanal before he became too deeply entrenched. It was to be but the first of several such attempts, always with ever larger forces, but always against an enemy who each time was proportionately stronger. This first attempt, Operation KA, was launched with the 1500-strong detachment under Colonel Ichiki, and, in order to soften up the American defences, 11 Air Flotilla was to subject Henderson Field to non-stop bombing. However, bad weather conditions ruled out these attacks for many days and only ten days' operations were possible during the 23-day preparation period. By 7 September a second airstrip had been built near Buin on Bougainville's south coast, with another to be built nearby at Kahili.

The Japanese air strength had increased steadily at Rabaul, from 153–173 aircraft in June 1942 to almost 600 by November 1942, the majority of them the navy's 11 Air Flotilla. The Army Air Force concentrated its strengths mainly in New Guinea with 4 Air Army at Wewak. By November 1943 the 24 Aichi D–3A2 'Vals' of 552 Kokutai (Air Group) had been supplemented by twenty of the sleek new Yokosuka D4Y1–C dive-bombers, code-named 'Judy', belonging to 501 Air Group. About fifty planes a month were flown in from Truk by the navy to keep numbers constant with losses. From time to time 300 extra aircraft of the Combined Fleet flew in to supplement the land-based aircraft at Rabaul.

Typical of the Japanese dive-bomber missions at this period was that of 1 August, during the initial stages of the New Georgia campaign that led to the fall of Munda to the Americans. Six fast US transports (converted destroyers – APDs) and five large landing ships (LCIs) were disembarking their troops near Baraulu Island early that morning. They had a screen of five destroyers and 32 fighters overhead. Despite this the Japanese dive-bombers achieved complete surprise when, at 08.30, a Red Alert was sounded over the anchorage and six Aichi 'Vals' approached the destroyer *Lang* while others headed for the navy's signal station at Bau Island. Two of the 'Vals' carried out their attack dives on the *Lang*, one of them releasing a single 550-lb bomb which exploded 300 yards off her port beam but caused no damage or casualties. Bombs exploded up and down the beach between Liana and Roviana island. One 'Val' was reported hit and to have crashed on New Georgia at the jungle edge. One of the protecting Marine Corps F–4U Corsairs was also hit by return fire and lost, but the pilot, Lieutenant Strudger Jnr, survived.

The short range of the single-engine dive-bombers used by both sides restricted their operations in the Solomons campaign, but this worked to the Americans' advantage. When the battle was being fought to take Henderson Field it was the Americans who were on the defensive and their Douglas S B Ds merely had to survive the nightly bombardments to be ready at dawn to take off. They then inflicted casualties on the Japanese infantry investing the strip or on the convoys running the gauntlet to reinforce them. The Japanese Aichi 'Vals', however, had to reach out to the extreme limit of their range in order to attack the strip or assist the Japanese attackers. Not surprisingly, casualties were heavy. The same applied to Japanese operations in support of their troops in New Guinea.

One Japanese dive-bomber mission, which took place in September 1942, can be considered typical of the problems which the young Japanese aircrew had to face even to reach their intended targets. At this time 'Vals' based at Rabaul were frequently mounting attacks in the Milne Bay area, at the eastern extremity of Papua, as the Australian and Japanese forces battled out the bitter Kokoda Trail campaign and the Japanese launched a twin assault, across the Owen Stanley range and from the sea.

The Australians rushed in reinforcements, several convoys of Dutch merchantmen carrying stores, supplies and troops being sent urgently to Port Moresby between May and August. On 24 August the Dutch freighter *Tasman*, laden with supplies from Port Moresby, sailed into Gili Gili to unload when word was received that a Japanese invasion convoy was on its way there. This, in fact, was the same Japanese invasion convoy that landed 1171 troops at Milne Bay on 25–26 August. Further reinforcements arrived the next night, all covered by naval forces and under cover of bombing operations mounted by 2 Air Corps from Rabaul. The Japanese force ran into strong resistance and had to be withdrawn.

The immediate result of the assault, however, was that the vulnerable Allied freighter was recalled and, to guard her, she was escorted by the brand new Australian destroyer *Arunta*. Once the crisis passed *Tasman* set sail again with *Arunta*. The two ships put into Milne Bay again on 2 September. Here they were spotted (as a light cruiser and a transport) and dive-bombers were launched against them.

The three-aircraft strike was led by a veteran Japanese navy flyer who had been recalled from retirement, Warrant Officer Ota Genga, with Yamakado Matae as his navigator. Genga had taken part in several of the earlier attacks against Milne Bay and knew the area well. His two accompanying aircrew, however, including Susumu Tanaka and Takeshi Maruyama, were young draftees with little or no combat experience. They had an escort of six Zero fighters but three hours after leaving Rabaul these were forced to break off, as their fuel was running low, and left the three dive-bombers heading south on their own.

They never arrived over Milne Bay, no Japanese air activity was reported there that day and no sightings were made by the two ships. What happened is a mystery but the next firm sighting of the three 'Vals' was from the air, on the beach at Table Bay, approximately midway between Abau and Milne Bay, on the southern coast of Papua. The aircraft were thought to have been damaged in combat but, as a party which reached the scene soon afterwards discovered, such was not the case. Each aircraft had been badly burned around the cockpit area by their own crews setting fire to their parachutes. Apart from this damage, however, the rest of the aircraft were in good condition. The least-damaged 'Val' was later recovered by barge and brought back for examination. The Japanese aircrew had taken their rear machine guns with them but the maps, documents and rations they were unable to carry were found buried at a camp site close by.

Native trackers eventually led Allied soldiers to the six airmen who were attempting to reach their own lines over the mountains; but at Dimuga they were cornered and three of them were killed in a brisk skirmish. The other three got clear, but not for long, because another patrol caught and killed them. The bodies were found to have proper walking boots, invasion money, steel helmets and concentrated rations as well as whis-ky! There was speculation that this was a special reconnaissance group who had put down deliberately, but this seems doubtful in the extreme. Most likely it was just another incident of how Japanese dive-bomber crews were dispatched in penny-packets against the Allies, and thus wasted in fruitless missions, instead of concentrating their power for massed dive-bomber assaults like the earlier one on Port Darwin. This policy would have given positive results and possibly swung the Papuan campaign their way.

Meanwhile frantic Japanese efforts to halt the relentless American pressure up the Solomon Island chain continued to sap their strength. On 13 August, for example, another transport *John Penn* was sunk by bombing off Guadalcanal and on 30 August eighteen Japanese aircraft hit Henderson Field, and a bomb from one of them sank the destroyer-transport *Calhoun*. But a further air attack on 8 September by the Rabaul-based aircraft against the troop transports *Bellatrix* and *Fuller*, running supplies into the American forces at Lunga Point, failed to achieve any hits on either vessel.

Vice-Admiral Jinichi Kusaka's 11 Air Flotilla had built up to a strength of some 220 aircraft to support the next attack but in heavy aerial fighting between 16 and 25 October these suffered very heavy losses to US Marine Corps fighters on Henderson Field.

During the desperate land attack on 26 October, led by General Kawaguchi, heavy hand-to-hand fighting almost led to the fall of Henderson Field; indeed at 02.30 a signal was dispatched by the General saying 'Henderson Field taken', but the positions could not be held in the face of fierce Marine counter-attacks and a force of fourteen fighters and many bombers, which had flown off their carriers to occupy the vital airstrip, circled it in vain until an attack by American fighters revealed that the strip was still in US hands.

On 11 November a heavy attack was made by 11 Air Flotilla on Henderson Field but, despite a number of fierce surface and air/sea battles in which the Japanese were often victors, the steady drain on their aircraft resources forced the withdrawal of the Japanese fleet in early November. For a while the new Japanese land force of the Hiroshima Division was forced to rely on land-based bombing support only. By mid-December, however, the development of a new airfield at Munda, New Georgia, was decided upon, along with a second one at Vila, south of Kolombangara, to neutralise Henderson Field and hold the rest of the Solomons Group. Rabaul still remained the main base from which both the attacks were planned and the evacuations executed and aircraft were routed southward along that island chain in a piecemeal fashion that left them vulnerable to attack.

The destroyer *De Haven* was bombed and sunk and the *Nicholas* damaged off Cape Esperance on 1 February 1943. They were part of a four-ship American destroyer unit attempting to stop the evacuation of Japanese troops from Guadalcanal during Operation KE, which followed up Operation KA.

Admiral Yamamoto committed the last, preciously husbanded, air reserves of Admiral Jisaburo Ozawa's carrier divisions of 3 Fleet to reinforce 11 Air Flotilla at Rabaul for one huge air strike, Operation I–GO, at the beginning of April 1943. No less than 65 Aichi D–3A1 'Vals' were flown in from the fleet's four carriers along with other aircraft and they joined the existing 27 'Vals' already based ashore. This great force was then thrown against the enemy.

In a mass attack launched against Allied shipping off Guadalcanal on 7 April 1943, the destroyer *Aaron Ward* was bombed and sunk in Lunga Roads, as was the New Zealand corvette *Moa* and the US oil tanker *Kanawha*, while another tanker and a transport were severely damaged. Again and again the dive-bombers dashed themselves against the wall of anti-aircraft fire and protecting fighters, and returned to their jungle strips in depleted numbers to bomb up, refuel and repeat the process. It was again a war of attrition they could not win. Another such attack was made on 11 April, against Oro Bay and Harvey Bay near Buna, New Guinea and was followed up the next day with a third attack, this time against Port Moresby itself. Milne Bay was hit on 14 April and another two transports were sunk. However, the returning Japanese pilots considerably over-estimated their successes, and their own losses, 49 aircraft in all, were worth more than the irritation they had inflicted on the Allies. The Japanese carriers were forced to withdraw to Japan to re-equip with men and machines.

When they returned to the fray with fresh aircrew the results were much the same. On 5 June an attack by 81 Japanese aircraft from Rabaul was met by 101 American fighters. A fierce battle took place over Russell Island in which 24 Japanese planes were destroyed for the loss of 7 American. On 16 June 1943, 94 Japanese aircraft from Rabaul and New Georgia attacked once more the Guadalcanal roadstead, sinking *LST 340* and the transport *Celeno* but failing to inflict any worthwhile hits on a large convoy. Another massacre resulted with only one of the Japanese aircraft surviving. On 9 July 1943 four American destroyers were actively bombarding Munda when they were attacked by 100 Japanese. Despite the odds the air attack was repulsed. Better results came, however, from a separate attack on a US landing force east of Lae, New Guinea, on 6 September: *LST 339* was sunk and the destroyer *Conyngham* and *LSTs 471* and *473* were damaged by bomb hits, despite early radar warning of the Japanese dive-bombers' approach.

With the establishment of the Buin airstrip on the southern coast of Bougainville operations by Japanese dive-bomber units became much more practicable. 26 Air Flotilla moved in to that base and was reinforced at the beginning of July 1943 by 2 Carrier Division under Rear Admiral Sakamaki. The Air Staff Officer, Commander Masatake Okumiyra, described the dive-bomber operations from Buin airfield in graphic terms:

Buin was a wretched air base, not comparable in airfield facilities to the enemy's magnificent engineering achievements. Our pilots had only one runway, 4000ft long and 800ft in width, running at right angles to the coast. Extending from each side of the airstrip were numerous small roads leading into the jungle, where we concealed the majority of our aircraft from aerial observation. Each night we moved every machine from the field into the jungle revetments and, during the day, did the same except for those ships which were on call. This dispersion kept our losses from enemy bombing and strafing to a minimum.

Our air force headquarters and sleeping quarters were located on the beach, approximately a mile and a half west of the field. Our

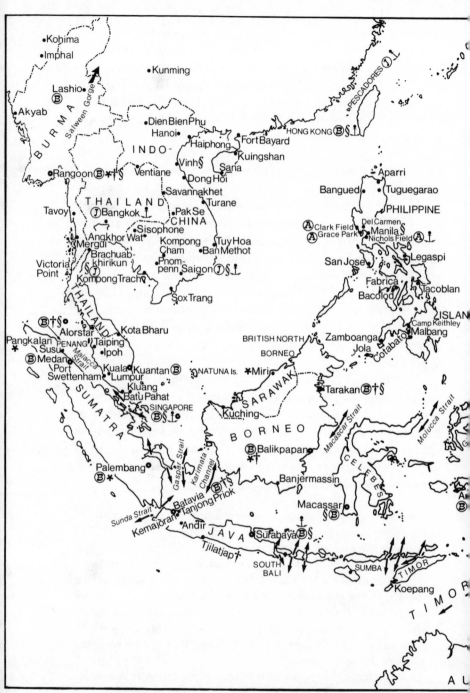

2 Strategic locations of SW Asia at start of the Jungle War, Dec. 1941

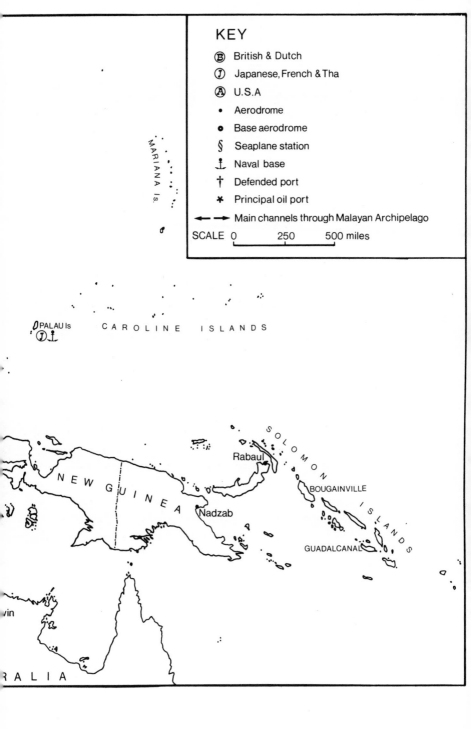

KEY

Ⓑ British & Dutch
Ⓙ Japanese, French & Tha
Ⓐ U.S.A
• Aerodrome
◉ Base aerodrome
§ Seaplane station
⚓ Naval base
† Defended port
✳ Principal oil port
◄——► Main channels through Malayan Archipelago

SCALE 0   250   500 miles

MARIANA Is.

PALAU Is

CAROLINE   ISLANDS

SOLOMON   ISLANDS

Rabaul

NEW GUINEA

BOUGAINVILLE

Nadzab

GUADALCANAL

RALIA

vin

'quarters' were simply barracks or, more accurately, tents scattered haphazardly over the ground. We raised the floors about six feet above the soil for protection against the severe heat and moisture.

The daily activity begins at the air base at least three hours before sunrise. In the steaming humidity, surrounded by insects, the mess crews begin the task of preparing meals for the day. Most of the maintenance crews also arise at this time to prepare the aircraft for the day's missions. The work of our mechanics is most strenuous, for they must bring all the aircraft which are to fly that day from their jungle revetments on to the field. One by one they are moved from the jungle cover, a band of men tugging and pushing the heavy aircraft over the soft ground. Everything must be done by hand; there is not a single tractor on the field. Two hours later, with sixty minutes yet to go before the sun shows over the horizon, the entire field awakens, and all men take their posts. The pilots and the aircrew members carry their flying gear to the assembly point which is the flight personnel pool near the runway. Here they eat their breakfast while they await the orders of the day.

The long day passes. The gathering dusk is a welcome sight, for it means some rest and, at least, respite from heavy raids. Neither we nor the enemy has the proper equipment to permit large-scale night attacks. Once the sun has set the aircrews, back from their missions, walk wearily to their respective sleeping quarters.

A second strip was utilised at Kolombangara Island, close to the actual ground fighting at Munda, in order to give better support and also to split the work load on the ground staff. Here conditions were even more primitive but some semblance of a base was maintained and it was used for as long as possible to stage attacks through from Buin. But it was still Buin that held the ring and was engaged almost daily in fierce fighting with the Henderson Field aircraft as well as those from New Guinea.

The next American thrust northward took place between 15 and 25 August when a strong landing force, 25 Division under Major-General McClure, was put ashore on the eastern coast of the central Solomon island of Vella Lavella. This by-passed the much stronger Japanese garrison which had been concentrated in readiness on Kolombangara. This assault was on Buin's doorstep and it was they that had to react to this fresh leap forward by the enemy. Accordingly they sent in what they had. The American convoy had already been sighted by a scout plane on the night of 14 August and, at first light, a force of 12 'Vals', led by Sub-Lieutenant Tachibana, took off to attack. They had an escort of no less than four dozen Zero fighters.

They were met by a force of 50 American fighters and a fierce skirmish took place over the beachhead. While the fighters entwined and grappled, the 12 Aichis tipped over and commenced their dives on the convoy below, being met with the usual intense hail of fire from the ships' guns, everything from 5in. shells through 40mm Bofors and 20mm Oerlikons with which all American ships now bristled. Into this hail of fire the D-3As threw themselves and released their bombs. Five of the Japanese dive-bombers fell in flames, including Tachibana himself, and three of their escorting fighters were also lost. In return they claimed to have sunk two big transports and one smaller freighter with direct hits and to have damaged four more of the convoy. Seven American aircraft were also thought to have been destroyed.

The attacks were resumed the same day, and no less than three assaults were made by the Buin-based aircraft, which included a total of 36 'Vals' in the 220 sorties flown, but in vain. The American landings proceeded without a hitch. Another rung in the Solomons ladder had fallen as the Americans pressed one step closer to closing the ring about Rabaul.

Constant outflanking attacks forced the abandonment of Buin in mid-October, 26 Flotilla moving back largely to Rabaul to join 25 Air Flotilla and being reinforced by, first, 1 Carrier Air Division (CAD) aircraft and then 2 CAD. From time to time the 'Val' dive-bombers were sent from Rabaul to operate from the Tripoiru airstrip north of Buin to give them a stopover and extend their range in order to strike at convoys and transports off Mono Island in the Treasury Group south of Bougainville. There were never more than twenty dive-bombers available at any one time for such raids and thus achievements were slight.

Nonetheless the Rabaul complex was still a tough nut to crack. On 12 October some 329 aircraft were in the area with five airfields in use: Lakunai and Vunakanua which had been seized during the original landings in January 1942, had been improved; Raporo was completed by December of the same year; while Keravat and Tobera were finished the following year. These fields were protected by 367 anti-aircraft guns with spotters and radio-location devices on strategic approaches to give early warning of attack in lieu of radar. Strong land forces and defence works completed the picture so it was not surprising that the Allies were to decide on a policy of by-passing rather than of direct assault, save from the air.

To neutralise Rabaul the US Army Air Force under General Kennedy launched a series of attacks, the first on 12 October by 349 aircraft, of which only four were lost. It should be noted, however, that the claims of the US airmen during this and subsequent attacks exceeded even the Japanese in their over-estimation of damage done and the almost farcical descriptions of damage inflicted. General MacArthur claimed that this one attack had knocked out Rabaul, that it was 'Pearl Harbor in reverse', and that 177 Japanese aircraft had been destroyed. Only 55 Japanese aircraft were lost from all causes at Rabaul during the whole of October, with another 35 lost the following month. Despite this, MacArthur's staff increased their claim that 732 Japanese aircraft had been destroyed or damaged and 138 ships sunk, including a heavy cruiser and seven destroyers. The true figures were 203 aircraft and one destroyer.

The relentlessness of the attacks meant, however, the attrition of Japanese aircraft over a period of time. Yet again, in order to replace losses, the six aircraft carriers of the 3 Fleet sailed from Truk to carry out Operation RO where their aircraft were landed ashore to partake of further air offensives against the Solomon Islands. By 1 November some 300 carrier aircraft had arrived and brought the total Japanese air strength at Rabaul to its peak of 550 planes, of which 390 were fighters. But further heavy Allied air attacks soon decimated these fresh arrivals. Nor did they achieve any more this time than before, for despite their optimistic claims not one major Allied warship had been sunk by them, and very few had even been damaged.

Far more severe, in terms of results achieved, than the Allied land-based air attacks were the attacks by the American carrier-borne aircraft of Admiral Halsey's fleet. On 5 November Rabaul itself was hit by strikes from the carriers *Saratoga* and

Princeton which damaged every ship of the powerful Japanese cruiser squadron anchored there, and only ten of the planes were lost.

On the night of 1–2 November further American landings took place with 37 Infantry Division disembarking at Cape Torokina. The 'Vals' from the fleet struck at a retiring American Task Force and damaged the cruiser *Montpelier* on 2 November. A strong force, which included 26 Aichi dive-bombers, mounted a further attack on 8–9 November against the transport anchorage and scored a hit on *President Jackson*. A second air attack the same day concentrated on the escorting cruiser squadron and the light cruiser *Birmingham* was severely damaged by both bomb and torpedo hits.

The two big American carriers returned to Rabaul on 11 November in company with reinforcements in the shape of *Essex, Bunker Hill* and *Independence*. This stung the Japanese into heavy counter-attacks. Along with 67 Zeros and 14 'Kates', some 27 'Vals' joined in the strike. Aboard one of the carriers a detailed eyewitness account of the counter-attacks was being recorded by Lieutenant Oliver Jensen, USNR:

> The attack began at 1.30 p.m. and lasted for an hour. The Japs attacked in three waves beginning with Aichi 99 dive-bombers. Fighters from *Essex* were taking off in the midst of it and shooting down Aichi 99s a few seconds later, even before they could retract their wheels for normal flying. Back on the carriers watchers at one moment counted eleven Jap planes burning on the horizon. The dive-bombing attack was followed by two waves of torpedo planes, then more dive-bombers. They threw in everything they had. Geysers splashed up all around the ships. There were many near misses. One burning dive-bomber apparently tried a suicide dive into *Essex* and, only a few seconds before hitting, exploded in a black burst of smoke and disintegrated. The wing fell separately, slower than the rest of the plane, and landed so close under the stern that men on deck could not see it hit.

Others took a more academic view of the Japanese dive-bombing techniques, including one of the Helldiver pilots, Rip Kline, who found himself stranded on the deck of *Bunker Hill* a few feet from his aircraft which was loaded with a 1000-lb bomb. He later gave Bob Olds a graphic description of his feelings:

> He found himself judging the skill of the enemy pilots. Rip watched the first bomb drops. He decided they would fall short. They did. The next bomb was more difficult to judge. Rip finally called it too long – it would overshoot the carrier. It did. Then came the pair that Johnny saw. The drop was really good, Rip thought in subconscious admiration. It was a sure hit. Then he realised the bombs were headed straight for him and would hit not far away. But the Skipper had given his order and the ship was turning.

The Americans claimed that 90-plus of the Japanese aircraft were shot down, but the actual losses were 33. The Japanese airmen in their turn claimed heavy damage inflicted on the Task Force but no American ship was hit and no American aircraft lost.

Under constant aerial bombardment the life of the shore-based 'Val' squadrons became nightmarish: lack of rest, lack of sleep, the continual drain of the climate, lack of spares, constant losses and the replacement of experienced men by recruits less able to maintain the high standards of their forebears; the knowledge that the endless sorties and losses had not succeeded in slowing down, let alone halting, the enemy who was seen to grow stronger despite his own losses. All this dragged the aircrew down but still they flew to almost certain death. Indeed when the question of relief came up it was almost regarded as an insult. As Okumiya recorded:

> I found in my discussion with 26 Air Flotilla flight personnel that they held the same impressions of futile combat, that further fighting could only postpone eventual defeat. The most astonishing reaction to 2 Carrier Division's arrival at Rabaul was that the knowledge that the flotilla could return to Truk did not engender relief. Instead, many of the flotilla's men could see only reproach in their replacement. They felt they were being removed from the front line because their performance was unsatisfactory, that the Navy expected 2 Carrier Division to accomplish what they had failed to do. An attitude of this nature is dangerous, for it can lead in a short time to the spiritual disintegration of even the strongest army.

The same fate now befell 2 Carrier Division. When, on 28 October, Admiral Koga had ordered the planes from 3 Fleet on to Rabaul's airfields they included 45 'Vals' in their strength. In the early November raids on the Bougainville beachheads the Japanese lost almost 75 per cent of their dive-bomber aircrews dead. On 12 November the carriers were again forced to return to Japan for fresh intakes of aircraft and green pilots and navigators. Of the 173 Japanese aircraft disembarked only 52 survived to return to their carriers at Truk a few weeks later.

The relentless American pressure continued with landings on New Britain itself of further large invasion forces. 1 Marine Division went ashore at Cape Gloucester on Boxing Day covered by a large Task Force. Again Japanese reaction was strong, on that day and the next a total of 300 aircraft were thrown against this beachhead and against a second which had been established on 15 December at Arawe on the southern coast. In the attack against Cape Gloucester some 60 Japanese aircraft took part only an hour after the landing started. A second attack followed later the same morning and then a third during the afternoon with a mixed force of both dive- and medium bombers directed against the covering naval force. The destroyer *Brownson* was hit and sunk in this attack and the destroyer *Shaw* (re-built after being blasted by 'Vals' at Pearl Harbor) was again heavily damaged and the destroyers *Drayton* and *Lamson* and *LST*s *66* and *202* also damaged. After this the attacks fizzled out and the Americans were again able to consolidate their positions. Another step forward.

This proved the last major effort of the land-based 'Vals' from Rabaul. The veterans had been lost in the island jungle fighting and it was with mere novices that the disastrous carrier battle of the Philippine Sea, the 'Great Marianas Turkey Shoot' that marked the end of Japanese air/sea power, was to be fought by the Japanese navy that coming June.

For the once-invincible 'Vals' of the Imperial navy the campaign in the Solomon Islands had indeed, as Masatake Okumiyra and Jiro Horikoshi also wrote, 'sucked our naval air forces, and ultimately our army and naval surface strength, into a bottomless swamp wherein waited only defeat'.

4
Counter-Strike

The arm of the Japanese thrust that had reached down the Solomon chain was complemented by a second, mainly composed of the Japanese 17 Army with its 6, 17 and 38 Divisions. It was deployed on the mainland of New Guinea and had, as its initial objective, the overland conquest of Port Moresby, on the southern coast. The Battle of the Coral Sea, in May 1942, had thwarted the seaborne attempt to capture it, but when the Japanese troops attempted to force the Owen Stanley range they were blocked; and after fierce fighting and the deprivations of the climate and the fever-ridden jungles, they were forced back. Finally, as in the Solomon Islands, it was the Allies' turn to inch their way forward but the determination of the enemy and the lack of their own resources made the going hard and difficult.

Thus, when the Australians held the first land-based Japanese thrust towards Port Moresby, it marked a significant turning point in halting Japanese progress southward just as had the US Marine landing at Guadalcanal. In both instances the Japanese initiative was first halted and then reversed, but in neither case was this initially apparent and it required much hard fighting before the Allies could go over to the offensive. The securing of Papua had priority but, once this was achieved and the Japanese attack on Wau beaten off, General MacArthur's thoughts turned to the more offensive operations embodied in the plan codenamed ELKTON to advance on Rabaul via New Guinea, New Ireland and New Britain. In the former area this required the seizure of Lae, Salamaua, Finschafen and Madang to provide jumping-off bases for the occupation of western New Britain.

As in all these campaign, but particularly so in New Guinea, close air support provided the key, giving the troops on the ground the essential, accurate heavy artillery support which the jungle and mountains made almost impossible by conventional methods. Naturally enough the dive-bomber was called upon to play the essential role in this. Make-do methods with Boomerang and Wirraway aircraft were all that was initially possible but soon the call went out for proper dive-bombers.

The Royal Australian Air Force did not begin to receive large batches of Vultee Vengeance dive-bombers until April 1943, a delay which was later to have severe repercussions. The RAAF classified this aircraft the A–27, but of the first 108 received by the end of that month only one-tenth were usable for initial training. The rest, for a variety of reasons, were unfit. 4 Operational Training Unit had been set up as early as October 1942 and was staffed with Australia's most experienced dive-bomber pilots as instructors, men like Doug Johnstone, Cyril McPherson, Berry Newman and John Gerber. The training they provided was of the highest standard.

Nonetheless when the aircrew reached New Guinea unforeseen problems were encountered. Air Vice-Marshal H. Scherger recalled later that they were obliged to spend much extra time on training when the group first moved to New Guinea, and, as time went on, the need for Forward Operational Training Units was to become more and more pressing. Scherger commented on the marked difference between American and Australian training methods. While the American pilots were given some operational training in the States, most of this type of learning was necessarily done in New Guinea itself where aircrew were 'blooded' by attacking relatively 'soft' targets, such as those in by-passed areas still in Japanese control. Only after this were they switched gradually to actual combat targets in the fighting areas. By then they had become used to both local conditions and enemy counter-action.

On the other hand the Australian method of giving the bulk of the training at home and then pitching fresh units straight into combat was found less satisfactory. A further problem was the constant lack of replacement aircraft at the period of highest combat activity. Political machinations behind the scenes both in Washington and London made the Australians' problems all the more complicated. Once a steady flow of aircraft did finally materialise it was too late.

Air Commodore (as he now is) E. G. Fyffe commented that the RAAF's dive-bomber strength was increased to meet training needs and generally the aircraft performed well, although casualties were suffered as was to be expected given the nature of the training and the experience of the trainees. The apparent main cause of accidents was the failure to recover from the dive due either to poor technique or elevator failures during or before the pullout phase. He added:

> In November 1943 I was appointed to command and form 77 Wing at Amberley, Queensland. 21 and 23 Squadrons were formed at Lowood while 24 Squadron, which had formed earlier at Bankstown, New South Wales, was sent to Dobodura, New Guinea. In December 1943 the HQ, plus 21 and 23 Squadrons also moved to Nadzab, New Guinea.

The Royal Australian Air Force squadrons had begun moving up into their operational areas in the late summer of 1943. The first was 24 Squadron, commanded by Squadron-Leader Barton Honey, which moved into New Guinea. A detachment of 18 Vengeances occupied Tsili Tsili on 2 September and started operations from there one week later. Their targets were enemy positions and occupied strongpoints holding up the Allied advance and the first strikes were at Finschafen and Lae. The American Air Force General, George C. Kennedy, had especially asked that dive-bombers be sent to New Guinea for use against difficult 'pin-point' targets in the Huon Gulf area. Unfortunately the squadron's detachment was originally seen as but a temporary one, and insufficient back-up stores and equipment were sent in to support the protracted air operations in which they soon found themselves involved.

On 7 September 1943, 24 Squadron was sent to attack a vital bridge on the Bogadjim road in order to cut off reinforcements to the enemy's forward battalions. This mission was aborted because of bad weather, however, the Vengeances having to jettison their bombs and almost running out of fuel on the return journey. An ignoble beginning for the squadron but they made amends by carrying out their mission successfully the following day. Unfortunately this was marred by the fact that they were heavily engaged by both American warships and fighter aircraft on their way to and from the target zone which, considering they were flying American aircraft, was disturbing. The resulting fall of Lae, however, somewhat compensated for their Allies' blunders.

On the morning of 18 September a strike by 14 dive-bombers was put in by 24 Squadron against targets around Finschafen. Attacks were pushed down to 1400ft and 500-lb bombs were used against gun positions, bunkers and occupied buildings. The Vengeances also strafed these targets on their way out, expending some 7000 rounds of ammunition. The potency of such methods was graphically demonstrated and the Army called for more.

The Vengeances then attacked enemy installations at Kakakoo and Salankau on 19 September 1943 and carried out strafing attacks, with both Flight-Lieutenant Richard R. Lewis and Flying Officer Ian G. Hunter claiming heavy casualties among the Japanese troops engaged.

Operations continued on 21 September with an attack on the Japanese radio location station on the islands of Kaial and Wonam in the Tami Group, off the coast from Finschafen itself. Although there was 7/10th cloud cover the dive-bombers dived down to 500ft, hit the station itself six times, and obliterated it. The only damage was to Flying Officer Jack Murray's aircraft which was hit by his own bomb fragments. Other bombs landing close by the main target wiped out machine-gun posts. Afterwards a signal was received from Colonel S. Davies of the US 5 Air Force: 'Congratulations on your highly successful strike against the enemy this morning.'

After an attack in the Finschafen area on 25 September another signal was received, this time from the ground forces: 'Troops exhilarated by your attack. Accuracy of aircraft on difficult targets enabled two companies to cross Bumi River.'

The pinpointing of the target was also confirmed by Lieutenant-Colonel A.R. Smith of the British Military

Mission who went ashore with the infantry battalion.

Number 24 Squadron itself now moved up to Dobodura to give close support to the Australian 9 Division in their amphibious assault at Sattelburg. On 28 September 1943 a force of 12 Vengeances spearheaded the actual assault landing at Langemak Bay. The subsequent report from the troops ashore was that the attack had been very effective. On 1 October the final assault went in, preceded again by the dive-bombers who pushed in so low that, again, one aircraft was hit by splinters from its own bombs.

At this period also a Vengeance of 24 Squadron, returning from a mission aborted because of bad weather against enemy barge traffic, Flight-Sergeant Keith B. 'Hank' Morgan, with Flying Officer Kenneth H. Pike as navigator, were flying at 7000ft over the coast when the engine misfire occurred and flames began to blow back from the engine cowling gill. For fifteen seconds the engine cut out completely and then it stuttered intermittently back to life, but continually misfiring. Oil and smoke kept pouring back from the engine, obscuring the pilot's vision. Morgan side-slipped out of formation and took his mount into a dive to try and extinguish the flames. He pulled out at 800ft with oil and flames still unabated and dumped his bombs. At once he made for the emergency air strip hard by the mouth of the Morobe River, losing altitude all the time. When still a mile from land and the runway itself, and at an altitude of only 100ft, Morgan tried lowering his flaps and, as he did so, the engine finally stopped.

There was nothing else left but to try to pancake on the sea, but a wave crest caught the Vengeance and flipped her up 30ft so that she nose-dived in at an angle of 35 degrees. Fortunately they were in shallow water, about seven feet. The two men managed to get clear of the cockpit and floated to the surface. Here they inflated their life-raft and got safely ashore, being rescued by an Australian AA-battery who returned them to the squadron a few days later none the worse for their ordeal.

During Japanese land attacks against the Australian 2/17 Battalion at Kumawa between 6 and 9 October 1943, 24 Squadron was called on to make repeated dive-bombing assaults on the enemy's main base at Sattelburg. The position became daily more precarious and, on 18 and 19 October, an all-out Japanese assault was broken only by repeated dive-bombing. During the final months of 1943, 24 Squadron was fully employed in a series of attacks on targets in New Britain and New Ireland, in particular against Madang and Alexishafen airfields.

The United States 5 Air Force, commanded by General George Kennedy, asked for a fully mobile Australian unit to operate in New Guinea. Ten Operational Group was set up in response and this included Fyffe's 77 Wing. It was initially planned that this force should go to Gasmata in southern New Britain and, from there, attack the by-passed Japanese garrison, but once the early results had been evaluated, a more active and relevant role was found for it.

In January 1944 the main parties of 21 and 23 Squadrons embarked aboard the *ss Van der Lijn* at Brisbane. As 24 (*City of Adelaide*) Squadron was already in the area it became the first operational third of the Wing and moved into Kiriwina early in December 1943 while 23 (*City of Brisbane*) Squadron became the second when it began moving into Nadzab in northern New Guinea. This strip, named Newton Field, had been established from virgin jungle by 62 Airfield Construction Wing, north of the river of that name. It comprised five separate, adjoining strips to the east, west and north-west of the village itself, bounded by mountains and by the Erap River to the west. This complex in the Markham Valley was to become 77 Wing's main base.

Number 23 Squadron was fully established there by February 1944. The final unit, 21 (*City of Melbourne*) Squadron, completed re-arming with the Vengeance at Gawler, South Australia. During its early adaptation of the Vultee the squadron was beset with considerable problems. As there had been no suitable site for a camp at Lowood, the equipment was dumped in a dry creak. Torrential rain followed, ruining all this gear and washing out the camp itself. The ground-crews were therefore unable to keep enough machines in a serviceable state to enable much training or practice to be carried out prior to the unit moving out to combat. This squadron began to move from Lowood with 23 Squadron in December 1943 and into Nadzab in January 1944. 18 of its Vengeances landed at Nadzab on 9 February direct from Lowood. On 10 February a familiarisation flight was conducted and on 11 February they began operations.

Twenty-four Squadron also began arriving, 15 Vengeances led by Squadron-Leader Honey landing there from Kiriwinda on Sunday 16 February. Their future targets were enemy strongpoints and gun positions holding up the advance of the Australian 5 and 7 Divisions moving along the Huon Peninsula in New Guinea. The latter division was at this time moving up the Rai coast in an attempt to join up with United States troops at Saidor but they were meeting fanatical resistance by the Japanese 20 Division, at a formidable barrier which was known to the troops as 'Shaggy Ridge'. It was against this fortress position that the RAAF Vengeances began their precision attacks with 24 Squadron on 17 January 1944. Like their companion squadrons in the Akyab and Assam, the Vengeance aircrew now became heavily committed to a bloody and pro-tracted slugging match. It was their accurate bomb delivery, substituting for the heavy artillery of the First World War, in an attempt to dislodge the well-dug-in enemy.

Number 24 Squadron took off from Nadzab at 09.45 and conducted their dive-bombing on the Kankiryo saddle, north-east of the Faria River which ran along the base of the Ridge. The Vengeances delivered some nine tons of bombs on this position, all the bombs falling in a line along the eastern slope. They followed this up with machine-gunning attacks.

Wing-Commander E. Fyffe arrived the next day to inspect the squadron. On 19 February 12 Vengeances took off at 09.55 and attacked the same position to soften it up prior to an assault by the 18 Brigade. This attack was a failure, however. Artillery should have provided spotting smoke for the dive-bomber pilots but, on arrival over the target, the relatively inexperi-enced pilots mistook the smoke laid down in advance by the defenders and delivered their bomb loads 800 yards from the enemy. One up to the defenders and a salutory lesson for 24

Squadron! Ironically the squadron itself was convinced that they had scored direct hits; they had, but not on the proper target.

During the night of 19/20 February heavy rain fell and another strike of twelve aircraft was dispatched against the first objective, Cam's Saddle, a 5000ft-high ridge leading at right angles up to Kankiryo itself. The rain continued and Honey had great trouble finding his target in the cloud and squalls that enveloped the hills. For twenty minutes, therefore, the squadron had to circle under anti-aircraft fire but Squadron-Leader Honey was determined not to be taken in again and bided his time until the Australian artillery shells began to indicate exactly where the enemy were. Precision dives followed down 1000ft through the murk and, at 200ft, some twenty-two 500-lb bombs, with 45-second delay fuses, were deposited, many of these directly on to the target which enabled the 2/10 Battalion to clear the saddle thereafter. Signals were subsequently received from the 7 Division: 'Direct hits on enemy positions. Accurate dive-bombing destroyed strong post on Green Snipers Pimple Ref 68246.' Another one from Area C read: 'Seven bombs seen to fall in target area – apparent difficulty in locating target due to smoke not rising. Brigade reports they were delighted with effort – could not have had any better attack.'

In a similar manner 24 Squadron supported the Army's next step forward on 22 January 1944. Again led by Squadron-Leader Honey, 11 Vengeances took off at 09.50 and delivered a further accurate consignment of bombs on target. The 2/12 Battalion was then able to take the feature known as McCaughey's Knoll. On 23 January they attacked targets near Kesawai, during a diversionary raid by the 12 Brigade. For once the weather was perfect and accurate attacks were made. By evening of the same day the Battle for Shaggy Ridge was won.

Next day the Vengeances bombed Japanese strong-points on the southern end of Gragat Island, Madang, returning in two groups. One aircraft, however, crashed on landing and was written off for spares. At 07.20 on 26 January 11 Vengeances were dispatched against enemy positions in the village of Ngada which they bombed through a hole in the cloud, scoring direct hits on some houses. That same afternoon they were placed on an alert in readiness to attack a reported Japanese destroyer, but nothing came of it save that A-27–227 taxied into a truck and knocked off its own wings, which were later repaired, however.

On 29 January 11 aircraft took off and dive-bombed enemy positions at Orgoruna and strafed the village itself in front of the Allied advance. There were no losses from enemy action but engine-failure on two machines resulted in the forced-landing of one of them ten miles from Newton Field, close to the river. This was the mount of Flight Lieutenant Louis A. Stevens and his navigator, Flight Sergeant H. G. Main. Three search parties were sent out to get them but none could get through the kuni grass; so food, nets and blankets were dropped to them by a Piper Cub light aircraft for the two days. Then the grass was burnt, which enabled the plane to land so that they could be rescued.

Next day a strike was made against the Yaula area as, again, the main target was obscured by cloud. On 31 January 1944, after a series of cancellations due to the weather reports being poor, 24 Squadron made a very effective strike on the Gori River Bridge at Bogadjim when the original target, 8 Road Bridge, on the Bogadjim road, was 'weathered out'. A force of six Vengeances, all that remained serviceable, were readied, as follows:

1	A–27–226	F/Lt Richard R. Lewis / F/Sgt M. Brown
2	A–27–250	P/O Stronack / F/Lt R. Brown
3	A–27–244	F/Sgt Barry / F/Sgt Gundersen
4	A–27–223	F/Sgt Debenham / F/Sgt Bamsey
5	A–27–241	F/Sgt Grefory / F/Sgt Kirk
6	A–27–52	F/Sgt Sellick / F/Sgt Cuthbertson

Each Vengeance carried two 500-lb demolition bombs with instantaneous fuses. Unfortunately Sellick's plane was forced to abort just before take-off due to a blown tyre. The weather was clear to the divide, then they hit 9/10 Cumulus, with visibility zero to 6000ft at Bogadjim and Madang. Over the original target itself they encountered 10/10 stratus with scattered cumulus from 3000ft to 6000ft. There was a large weather front to the north-west of Madang, with visibility from five to ten miles over the target. The report stated flatly that the primary target was completely closed in by the weather. Not surprisingly, therefore, of the five aircraft actually dispatched, two failed to find the target. These released their bombs near to some huts near Bogadjim itself.

At 10.28, led by Richard Lewis, the remaining three aircraft began their dives from 2500ft through the heavy flak the Japanese had assembled to protect this vital link. This was described as being 'moderate, light, inaccurate' from the southern approaches of the bridge and it was estimated that the enemy had five or six guns positioned there. The aircraft pressed in as low as 800ft–400ft in their determined assault and scored four direct hits on the bridge itself, demolishing it, while two gun positions alongside were also wiped out. They also strafed the approached to the bridge, and Baumonna village, expending 5750 rounds of .30 ammunition. Again the only damage, to two of the Vengeances, came from their own bomb explosions, but all returned to base.

A short rest spell followed for 24 Squadron. Training was conducted for fresh intakes of aircrew at Lake Wanum as the conditions encountered in New Guinea bore no resemblance to South Australian OTUs. Meanwhile the other squadrons were arriving in support and so, after re-grouping, the dive-bombers went into action once more.

At 09.00 on 7 February, 24 Squadron's Vengeances co-operated with the Army by spotting for the artillery, and then went on to make another attack on the Gori River Bridge with six planes. Once more it was obscured by cloud and, instead, the strike was directed, rather ineffectually, against a small village. Six planes of 23 Squadron and six from 24 Squadron were bombed up on 9 February but the mission was cancelled and a test flight was made on the following day with Fyffe and eight of 23 Squadron's aircraft flying up the valley to Gusap to se if this strip could be used regularly as an operational field rather than just an emergency fuelling strip. The muddy conditions they found there seemed to rule this out.

On 11 February 1944 six planes from 24 Squadron, under Flight Lieutenant Richard R. Lewis, and six more from 23 Squadron on their first combat mission, were led by Wing-Commander T. R. Philp, DFC, against Yoga Yoga village. American troops at Saidor had reported that the enemy was using these native villages as staging posts as they retreated back to Bogadjim, and asked for them to be taken out. Arriving over the target at 08.05 to find the usual cloud, they nonetheless pushed down through it to deliver a low-level attack. The twelve dive-bombers scored several direct hits and flushed out almost a hundred enemy troops, although 300 had got clear just prior to the attack.

On 12 February 1944 occurred a repeat attack with 12 Vengeances of 23 Squadron and six from 24 Squadron to help 7 Division. Again poor weather spoilt the main mission target, so attacks were delivered on the area between Bridges 13 and 14 on the Bogadjin road. Bombing was recorded as 'poor' with only two aircraft scoring direct hits. Eighteen dive-bombers were dispatched against a small village close to Madang which was wiped out. A low-level attack was also made at 10.00 the next day on the villages of Tarikngan, Gwarawan and Yoga Yoga, south of Saidor, 2400 rounds of ammunition being expended in strafing runs.

Bambu village was bombed the next day by six Vengeances of 24 Squadron and on 16 February both units hit the same region once more. Numerous similar attacks followed as the enemy started pulling back both against troop concentrations and the Japanese-held airstrips at Alexishafen and Madang. The former was attacked on 17 February.

The pattern was now well established, with daily missions and the squadrons gaining in expertise. Nonetheless there was a remorselessness to it all, a non-stop pounding away at a hidden and resilient enemy with little positive to show for the squadron's skill and dedication other than the enthusiastic reports of the front-line troops about how their accuracy was helping them advance and, at the same time, minimising their losses.

On the next raid nine Vengeances attacked shipping and AA-batteries at Hansa Bay, refuelling at Gusap on the way.

They encountered lots of accurate light flak and some heavy batteries. Lewis had his own bombs hang-up on him and his undercarriage leg stuck as well. Despite this he got down safely. The same planes returned the following day and managed temporarily to silence the batteries with six hits. It was confirmed subsequently that two heavy guns had been destroyed and three others badly damaged. On Sunday 20 February, the dive-bombers' target was a Japanese supply dump at Aiyau which was hit by eight bombs and destroyed and on the following morning strafing attacks were again made against Saidor.

Reinforcements were on their way to relieve them of some of the pressure. Number 21 Squadron had arrived at Nadzab on 18 February, thus bringing the Wing up to full strength. After a short spell this third squadron could now join in the massed dive-bomber assaults, and they thus made their debut on 22 February 1944 when three of its aircraft joined with 23 and 24 Squadron machines in attacks on Japanese supply barges hidden on the Wagol River, Madang. Saidor was attacked next day in dives from 10,000ft, one bomb from each Vengeance being dropped in the first dive and the second during a follow-up glide attack. Of the 20 bombs dropped by the 10 aircraft, 19 were direct hits according to a congratulatory signal from the US 6 Army.

Twenty-three Vultees from 23 and 24 Squadrons made a heavy assault on the Japanese anti-aircraft positions located at Hansa Bay Cape Gloucester on 24 February, but for the first time they took casualties when two Vengeances fell to fierce anti-aircraft fire which machine-gun attacks by Kittyhawks had failed to silence. Flying Officer N. G. Burnell's machine, with Captain W. P. Watson, the Army Liaison Officer as passenger, was preparing to dive, with bomb-bay doors already open, when it was hit. The aircraft could not pull out of its dive and exploded on crashing into the sea about 300 yards from the target. The second machine hit, that of Flight Sergeant F. G. McDonald, with Flying Officer C. McAllister as his Observer, was seen to be hit by gun fire. Their plane went down just off the coast and although they were both seen to reach the shore they were not heard of again.

Madang and Alexishafen were bombed once more by 23 and 24 Squadrons on 27 February, while the next day nine Vengeances from 24 Squadron attacked Madang strip and 21 and 23 Squadrons Alexishafen. All three units bombed supply dumps and barges at Madang yet again the day after.

And so the grinding down of the unseen enemy continued without pause or respite. Indeed, as a major facet of the continual attempts to keep the enemy airstrips neutralised pending General Douglas MacArthur's attack on the Admiralty Islands, planned for 29 February 1944, the three RAAF Vengeance squadrons, 21, 23 and 24, kept up a round-the-clock pounding of airfields.

The RAAF dive-bombers therefore launched an all-out effort, beginning on 26 February: 21 and 23 Squadron then launched a major strike against the Japanese No 1 airstrip at Alexishafen. Simultaneously another 12 Vengeances from 24 Squadron bombed the Madang airfield, while the next day the same two targets were again subjected to similar dive-bombing assaults. Thirty-three Vengeances from the Wing were dispatched to attack both the airstrips at Alexishafen and the one at Madang again on 28 February despite the fact that the damage caused by the previous two days' bombing was apparently still not fully repaired. The Vengeances of 24 Squadron remained over Madang itself for some twenty minutes, strafing at low level anything that looked like a worthwhile target.

On 2 March 1944 two dozen dive-bombers attacked enemy positions on Karkar Island. In their approach to the target 23 Squadron climbed to 13,000ft, then they quickly formed into line astern and dive-bombed the mission house at Kurum and flattened the villages, following this up by machine-gunning with front and rear guns at low level. Save for light AA-fire, there was little sign of the enemy.

On 3 March 1944 the Vengeances undertook further close-support missions at Mindiri, New Guinea, between Saidor and Bogadjim where US troops were going ashore in an attempt to cut off the retreating Japanese. Both 23 and 24 Squadrons attacked the village itself and a camp at nearby Herwarth Point. On the morning of 4 March the dive-bombers from all three

Australian squadrons hit an enemy concentration at Pommern Bay close by. They returned for a second strike that same afternoon, the only casualty being one Vengeance which force-landed on return to base, but the crew was rescued. With their aid the American infantry took Mindiri the next day.

A maximum strike by 36 dive-bombers from all three Australian squadrons was mounted against the enemy-held village of Rempi, ten miles to the north of Alexishafen on the morning of 8 March. Number 24 Squadron's contribution to this mission (Madang Special No 1) was 12 aircraft deployed but 13 were actually utilised, as follows:

A–27–276	F/Lt Richard R. Lewis / F/O Cooper
A–27–240	F/Sgt Shaw / F/Sgt Follent
A27–74	F/O Hunter / F/Sgt Baker
A–27–222	F/O Roberts / F/O Robinson
A–27–52	F/Sgt Mammatt / F/Sgt Burns
A–27–291	F/Sgt Ellis / F/Sgt Stirling
A–27–241	F/Lt Baldwin / F/O Walsh
A–27–243	F/O Stansfield / F/Sgt J. M. T. Brown
A–27–244	F/Sgt Griffin / F/Sgt Parsloe
A–27–58	F/Sgt Morgan / F/O Pike
A–27–242	F/Sgt Smith / F/O Dalliston
A–27–75	F/Sgt Bannister / F/O Sparks
A–27–86	F/Sgt Sellick / F/Sgt Cuthbertson

They were airborne at 10.32, lifting off through the hot, sticky humidity and gaining height. The weather conditions were very poor, 8/10 cumulus, with base at 1000ft, tops at 6000ft, and a large rain front was encountered moving south-east, with its base at 1000ft and its tops extending up to 12,000. As a result heavy rain was falling throughout the whole of the attack. Indeed 23 Squadron was unable to hit the target, dropping its bombs north of the village itself. Two possible barges were sighted moored just off the beach but they were not attacked.

Using shallow dives because of the low cloud base the other two squadrons were much more successful. Number 24 Squadron attacked at 11.50 hours and dropped 24 500-lb demolition R/E bombs, while two others were brought back due to the

failure of the select switch to arm the fuses. The pilots subsequently reported that 'eight bombs had burst amongst the
Mission buildings which appeared to have been burnt out prior
to the attack. Two bombs fell in the sea and two bombs fell on
the beach, others were unobserved. The Mission was obscured
by dust and smoke, making damage unassessable, the area was
strafed.' Some 4800 rounds of ammunition were expended.
Four of the Vengeances were holed by AA-fire, which nonetheless was reported as slight, medium and accurate, with the
shells bursting from 5000ft to 6000ft and of the tracerless
variety so that it could not be seen coming. One of the damaged
aircraft took four days to repair but there were no actual losses.
A repeat strike was ordered for the following day but it was
never delivered as the weather grounded all aircraft at Nadzab
and, by the time it had cleared, a bombshell from their own side
had struck them.

After their return from this impressive strike a signal was
received from MacArthur's headquarters. It stated bluntly and
without warning that 77 Wing was to cease all operations
forthwith and return to Australia. After all their great efforts
and their impressive achievements this seemed, to most of the
Australian dive-bomber crews at Nadzab, like a blow in the
face.

Air Vice Marshal F. R. W. Scherger, 10 Group's Commander, was unfortunately absent in Australia when this order
came through. Group-Captain C. W. Pearce, his second-in-
command, duly notified him of what had taken place, but when
Scherger tried to see Major-General Ennis C. Whitehead of
US5 Air Force to inquire the reason for this decision, he was
told that Whitehead could not be disturbed. And that was the
end of all argument although Scherger was later to discover that
Allied HQ and RAAF Command had already agreed to the
American decision beforehand. He therefore had no choice but
to comply.

The official reason was later given as a combination of the
inefficiency of the Vengeance (due to its limited range, engine
problems and two-man crewing), the large numbers of modern
American machines available to the US 5 Air Force (including

numerous less accurate but *single*-seater fighter-bombers), and
the lack of airfield accommodation at Nadzab and other New
Guinea airfields. The official Australian historian mentions the
fact that the Vengeance was requiring the full 6000ft of runway
at Newton to get airborne and that Kittyhawks could carry the
same bombload and act as fighters if attacked. He added:
'However, most of the Vengeance crews realised the shortcom-
ings of the aircraft they flew and were resigned to the decision.'
Even Scherger himself commented that, 'it was merely the
yardstick of efficiency which decided the question'. Some
British apologists take the same line, one stating that 'the
resulting loss of accuracy could be accepted'. These views have
not, however, been subscribed to by many of the Vengeance
pilots with whom I have been in contact. General Kennedy
informed the RAAF that he would not wish to employ the
Vengeances any more anywhere in the south-west Pacific.
However, as one American historian later admitted, 'Dive-
bombing, early advocated by General Billy Mitchell and fun-
damental to Navy tactics, found little support in the Army Air
Corps.'

The only Australian Vengeance pilot who expressed any
support for this viewpoint was John Gerber, who says: 'In
summary, the role and employment of the Vultee Vengeance
aircraft in the RAAF could best be described as a misuse of
resources.' The majority of others, on the other hand, disagree
with American conclusions on this point. Cyril McPherson
added his own, more intimate findings in a letter he wrote at the
time to the press but which he never dispatched:

I was instructing at 4 (Vengeance) OTU at that time and had
occasion to speak to a few of these pilots, some of them immediately
on their return from New Guinea. Those I spoke to were, for the
most part, more than satisfied with the aircraft's performance and
were keenly disappointed that the squadrons had been withdrawn
after such a short period in operations. I am also amazed at the
claim that pilots were using the full length of Newton Field runway
to become airborne. When I was in Merauke in Dutch New Guinea
(now West Irian) with 12 Squadron, we operated off a 3000ft
airstrip and our pilots, applying the recommended 15-degrees of

flap, experienced no difficulty in taking off with a full bomb load under similar conditions to those which would have applied at Newton Field, Nadzab. Certainly the Vengeance had limited range, but so did the fighters (which were subsequently used as fighter-bombers to replace them) until they were fitted with auxiliary fuel tanks. If such tanks had been fitted under the Vengeance wings, the range could have been very substantially increased, and it would have still been able to deliver a load of 1000-lb bombs. On this point, whilst my recollection is that the Vengeance's operational endurance was rated at about 3–1/4 to 3–1/2 hours, 12 Squadron's aircraft were frequently required to carry out anti-submarine patrols and shipping escort operations which required them to be airborne for more than four hours. My logbook shows that I flew one such operation of 4 hours 20 minutes and several others ranging from 4 to 4–1/4 hours. To achieve this pilots had to lean out their fuel mixture and throttle back below normal cruising speed, which was not important if one was simply stooging around a convoy keeping an eye out for submarines.

Regarding the claim that there were repeated cases of engine failure with Vengeance machines I must say that I never heard of any cases of engine failure among the Vengeance squadrons in New Guinea. The author may have been misled by reports of considerable trouble with Vengeance reconditioned engines which was experienced subsequent to the withdrawal of the squadrons from New Guinea.

Whatever the rights or wrongs of the decision the withdrawal of 77 Wing left only 25 (*City of Perth*) Squadron which had earlier re-equipped with the Vengeance at Fremantle, West Australia. They were utilised on coastal patrol work from mid-1943 onward, and, being the last operational Vengeance unit, became the only one to re-equip with the much superior Vengeance IV. However, it saw little or no combat other than to carry out anti-submarine patrols and be involved in the Australian invasion scare of 7 March 1944, when a report by an American submarine of two Japanese heavy units, which it was assumed were battleships, steering south from Singapore caused a massive 'flap'.

The Vultee Vengeance lingered on in the RAAF into post-war service but mainly as a target tug. Their operational period at Nadzab can now be seen as a great if limited achievement, and one that remained unfulfilled. Even better results would have been achieved had the RAAF been allowed to continue close-support work with the Vengeance. As it was, the RNZAF and the USMC had to take up the banner and continue the work; but the irony was that they used an older, slower and inferior machine for the job while the new, much improved, marks of the Vengeance languished in secondary roles.

5
Across the Imphal

Number 84 Squadron RAF was a Blenheim light bomber squadron, one of several flown in from the Middle East during the desperate days of the initial Japanese advances in 1942. Operating from Java, it was practically wiped out within a short period and the survivors reached India by devious routes only after hair-raising adventures. The squadron was saved from extinction, however, by Squadron-Leader Arthur M. Gill, the senior surviving officer. Through his efforts the unit was rebuilt and became one of several ultimately re-equipped with the long-awaited new Vultee Vengeance dive-bomber. But it was a long process.

Once they had been re-equipped, however, 84 Squadron had also to re-train and learn about dive-bombing, a subject which had been largely ignored in the RAF during the previous twenty years. Under pressure of dire necessity, therefore, they had to work out their own tactics and methods 'on the wing', as it were, and while still learning the squadron was sent to Ceylon for a period because of the fear of another carrier strike by Japanese naval task forces like the one in April 1942 which had caused such havoc. Much of 84 Squadron's work was therefore directed against shipping targets before they later returned to the Indian sub-continent to train in the army close-support role, which had been their original task.

As a result it was not until December 1943 that 84 Squadron completed its period of enforced 'back-area' duty which the arrival of the monsoon season had prolonged. Since 19 August the unit had been based in northern India at the airfield of Ranchi, in Bihar. Here they had not been idle, for an intense period of training had been undertaken to work out the details of close-support strikes but this time in conjunction with the army. When the weather in the Arakan lifted 84 Squadron again prepared themselves to move forward and an advance party was dispatched to Chittagong on the north-west edge of the Bay of Bengal (in what is now Bangladesh). On arrival this group purchased a large brood of hens in readiness for the squadron's Christmas dinner but, two days before the bulk of the unit was due to follow them, the Air Officer Commanding 221 Group flew to Ranchi to tell them that they had been selected to support Major-General Orde Wingate's Long Range Penetration Group (3 Indian Division) on their forthcoming mission far behind Japanese lines in Burma. On 6 December, therefore, the Squadron moved to Maharjpur, in Gwalior, and started two months' more intensive training with the Chindits.

The new penetration by Wingate's troops, code-named Operation THURSDAY, had been mooted as long ago as the Quebec Conference which Wingate himself had secretly attended. 10,000 men were to be airlifted in gliders over the Chindwin river and deposited at secretly prepared airstrips – code-named Aberdeen, Chowringhee and Broadway – in the hills of the upper Irrawaddy near Henu and Katha. They were to be kept supplied by Dakota transports and were to strike at the vital railway line connecting Mandalay in the south with the Japanese forward northern garrisons at Myitkyina. The latter was itself the objective of the American General 'Vinegar' Joe Stilwell's column moving down from the Himalayan mountains and across the Hukawng Valley to Kamaing. Various strategic points on that railway were to be cut – Indaw, Henu, Hopin – and a bolder stroke was later made east to Bhamo. Between 15–23 March 1944 the plan was put into effect. Such boldness depended utterly on Allied control of the air and the ability to respond quickly by accurate bombing in close support of the troops. Hence the intensive training of the previous December and January.

Wingate had said to Squadron-Leader Gill, 'If I give you a map reference of a target I want obliterated fast, can you bomb it?' As both the RAF and the Army used the same maps for this operation, so that there would be no confusion, the task seemed easy when expressed like that; but Gill recalled, in a series of interviews with me in the spring of 1985, how pointing at a

mark on a map and identifying that point in the jungle from the
air are two entirely separate things. He therefore replied to
Wingate honestly: 'No, we can't . . . if you have a target here
I'm not going to be able to see it unless you get it photographed.'
This Wingate could not do at that time as there was a shortage of
photo-reconnaissance aircraft in Burma.

Gill added that it was no good just giving him a map
reference, or a latitude and longitude, for jungle bombing if
accuracy was required. The dive-bombers could hit anything,
provided they were sure of what they were aiming at; the target
therefore had to be identified by the troops on the ground. Gill
asked for smoke marking. Wingate snorted. If he could lay
down smoke then so could the Japanese and the RAF would
not be able to tell which was which. And smoke, anyway, would
drift away.

All right, Gill replied, lay it down in a pre-determined
pattern, triangular or rectangular, change the smoke colour
day by day, then we will bomb only what we recognise. So they
worked and practised, tested and talked. Wingate was eventually won round by the eager and dedicated dive-bomber pilots.
But it took time.

The reasons are not hard to find. Over the previous years of
war the Army had been ill-served by the RAF in the field,
many would say grossly neglected. Without a precision instrument like the dive-bomber British air support had mainly
arrived too late or been misplaced. Almost always it was
ineffective. The soldiers did not trust the RAF to bomb close to
the front-line in the way that German troops had always taken
for granted with the Stukas. In many ways the dive-bomber
crews had to earn the suspicious infantryman's trust. Arthur
Gill added this rider:

> This is true enough, although in Burma the time had come when
> they were so desperate and hard-pressed that they would call up the
> air forces. I think that what worried me was that many times
> they told me that the enemy were within one hundred yards of our
> front-line troops. That is very close for bombing, even dive-
> bombing. The only way then that you could accept a target like that
> was by bombing parallel to our lines. We'd say, 'Well show me

exactly where the front line is and confirm that we have not got any troops further east than that point'. They would do so and we would find and identify the target and the British troops, and then we would bomb parallel to them, so that any overshoots from drift – and this was usually longitudinal, you would very seldom get a lateral drift – would fall clear of our own boys but still among the Japanese. Dive-bombing, of course, was the natural method for this sort of thing. In fact I remember that on one target we had a signal that said, 'Japanese commander in north-east room of house', which amused us and seemed a trifle optimistic, but it serves to show what the Army ultimately came to expect of dive-bombers by then.

Just how Wingate finally came to think of the dive-bombers after these prolonged training sessions and tests was shown in a letter from the Supreme Commander, South-East Asia, Lord Louis Mountbatten, sent to Squadron-Leader Gill on 18 January 1944:

I was so impressed by the bearing and enthusiasm of your officers and men and by your own desire to get back into action as soon as possible that I immediately took up the question of your Squadron's future with the Air Commander-in-Chief. Bearing in mind that General Wingate has formed such a high opinion of 84 Squadron and was so anxious to have you with him, I pressed Sir Richard Peirse to allow you to go forward into battle and I know you will be glad to hear that he has agreed.

And so 84 Squadron went to war.

A summary of 84 Squadron's operations from late February to early March 1944, gives some idea of the scale and intensity of their dive-bombing in support of 4 Corps:

Date	Number of aircraft	Target
16–2–44	16	Tawzi to Manhon road
18–2–44	–	HQ at Kuntawng
20–2–44	12	Metkalet (aborted by base)
23–2–44	12	Metkalet
24–2–44	–	Tullihal (exercise)

25–2–44	6	Hmawyonmaing
26–2–44	12	Troops south of Chaung
26–2–44	–	Troops S.E. of Paungbyin
27–2–44	–	Tonzi
29–2–44	12	Metkalet
1–3–44	12	Paukpyin
3–3–44	12	Pinelebu

The main danger to the British dive-bombers was from light AA-fire. Interception by Japanese fighter aircraft never took place and the enemy were unable to bring up heavy AA-guns to such forward positions. Thus the dual-purpose 75mm M88 gun was only rarely encountered by Vengeance aircrews. More common was fire from such weapons as the 6.5mm Taisho 3, nicknamed 'The Woodpecker' by the Allies. Introduced back in 1915 it was still standard equipment and could be used on a mounting as an AA weapon. It could also be fitted with wheels to negotiate difficult terrain, which made it ideal for Burma fighting. The Japanese army also frequently used the 13mm heavy machine-gun against low-flying aircraft. Arthur Gill recalls:

> The Japanese were experts at digging bunker positions deep down. They'd dig a deep hole and lay logs over it then put all the soil that they had dug out over the top of that. This made direct hits the only thing that would penetrate them. Our bombing evidently worked all right. We used delayed-action bombs in addition to instantaneous bombs, and the anti-personnel 500-lb Nose Instantaneous Tail Instantaneous (NITI) bombs with 9cm or 12cm rods on them, which meant that directly the rod hit the ground the bomb would spread shrapnel around. The others were General Purpose (GP) bombs which dug themselves in a bit before exploding. Then of course we also dropped 5-second and 10-second delayed action bombs – and up to 12-hour or 24-hour delay. A small time delay meant that the bomb would act as a semi-armour-piercing (SAP) missile and burrow itself into a bunker before detonation and in fact one of the signals we had back from the Army later confirmed that they had made a body count of 265, which they later revised to over 450, dead Japanese and that was from only one strike. So it was working and this knowledge helped us to plan other missions.

Despite gloomy predictions by the theorists in Whitehall and elsewhere, Vengeance losses remained minimal. One of the few took place on 4 March 1944. 84 Squadron had been sent to attack a concealed Japanese camp in the jungle north of Kontha. Each Vengeance was equipped for this mission with two 500-lb bombs, one 250-lb incendiary bomb, and one 250lb NITI bomb. Led by Arthur Gill they arrived over the target area after some twenty minutes' flying time from Kumbhirgram and found visibility down to only one or two miles. Despite this they tipped over into the dive and registered direct hits on the target area. On return to base, however, another strike against the same target was considered essential, which required quick re-arming. As Gill said, 'It would take less than an hour to complete a turn-round and be off again. Refuel and the bombs would be already fused. And sometimes you put in your reserve crews.'

On this occasion Gill's usual navigator, Flight Lieutenant Hawke, flew the first mission but Flight Lieutenant Blackburn flew with him on the second strike. A Motor Transport (MT) driver with 84 Squadron was H. Widdop who gave a good insight of the ground personnel's part in these intensive operations when recalling them for me:

Number 84 Squadron had three petrol bowsers at base, two Bedfords and one International. The Bedfords had a small JAP engine in a rear compartment which had to be started for pumping the Octane up to the aircraft, but the International was controlled by using a lever in the driving cab, a much easier way to do it. As soon as the aircraft reached the dispersal area and switched off 'all' after a raid the Aircraft Fitter was ready for refuelling. This was one of the first jobs to do as no condensation was allowed to get into the aircraft's fuel tanks – 100 Octane was always used. While filling the tankers at the petrol dump a stand-pipe was used to put into each 40-gallon drum, making sure that it never sucked the bottom of the drum where there would be grit etc. I don't know for sure how the drums arrived at the petrol dumps as I never saw them arrive by air or even by road from Silchar, which was the most likely source.

Refuelling VVs was fairly quickly accomplished until a new order was issued to the effect that we had to use a sort of bucket with a spout at the bottom to fit in the aircrafts' tanks and also three wires were fitted with clips which we had to clip to parts of the aircraft as a sort of earthing device. Furthermore a chamois leather was supplied to fit on top of the bucket which had to be cleaned regularly. Our Engineering Officer, Flight Lieutenant Ramsden, saw to it that we kept using these contraptions although it made a slower job of refuelling.

A few times the Squadron had to take off at first light and it was a grand sight seeing them lifting up with their exhausts firing and sometimes, when returning, to find low clouds covering the landing strip. After flying above the clouds for a while they would find their way down and land safely. Many a time I had to go round the Squadron's aircraft, even after the engine run-up, just to top up the fuel tanks with a extra pint or so during long-range missions to help the Chindits. These were orders because on such deep-penetration sorties every drop was essential.

As for personalities the squadron had a great many of them. Flight Lieutenant Johns was an Australian in charge of 'B' Flight. He went on raids dressed like General Patton with a slouch hat, six-shooters and a dagger. An American pilot, W/O Q. A. Keech, had a pint too many one Christmas and wanted to fly his Vengeance through the squadron goal posts, but as he could not get the engine covers off in his condition, he had to give this idea up. Our French-Canadian pilot once came in to land without his undercarriage down, despite repeated warnings. Afterwards he said that, with the loud screeching in his ears as his belly slid along the strip, he could not tell what he was being told on his radio.

Arthur Gill also remembers Keech:

We had only two Americans flying with our squadron. One of them was Keech who was a Warrant Officer who had joined the RAF. So although he was an American he had come over to England and joined up quite voluntarily. He wasn't an American serviceman. In all we had a mix of ten nationalities in 84 Squadron, two Americans, 56 Australians, some Canadians, a French-Canadian (more French than Canadian), Rhodesians, New Zealanders and of course some Irish, Welsh and Scots mixed in with the English, but we all jelled OK. The Aussies would call us 'Pommie Bastards' and we'd call them 'Aussie Creeps' or something less printable, but in those more tolerant days nobody made a fuss about such things.

'Curly' Keech, inevitably so-named because of his severe American crew-cut, flew with the second strike on this occasion, with Warrant Officer E. R. Watkins as his Navigator/Wireless Operator/Air Gunner in Vengeance 'V' for Victor. Once more the dives were made accurately and direct hits were again registered but this time there was some light flak hosing up to meet them. Keech's plane never pulled out of its dive and the distinctive oily burst of the Vengeance impacting later showed up on the photographs of the strike clearly amidst the normal bomb explosions on the target. Both crew members were killed instantly, their loss being recorded as 'possibly due to AA-fire from the ground', although they would never be certain. Watkins had a small black-and-white mongrel called Snaggles with him as on most of his missions.

Two dozen Vengeances, 12 from each squadron, went out on 8 March 1944 and hit Sakhan. Next day, owing to the change in the tactical situation on 4 Corps' front, both 84 Squadron and 110 Squadron were placed at the disposal of 23 ASC (Army Support Command). This brought forth a comment in the Wing's Record Book: 'It is hoped that the lessons learned when this Wing were last working for the ASC will be remembered, viz. that it is unfair for Vengeance pilots to be given pin-points in the jungle as targets without any photographs or smoke indication.'

Le–U was the target on the next combined attack by the Vengeance squadrons, both mounting two attacks each with 22 machines from 110 Squadron and 23 from 84 Squadron. On 11 March the targets were more diverse, 84 Squadron striking at Gwengu and Nyaungbintha with six planes on each mission, while 110 Squadron was hitting Nanbon and Tanga with the same numbers of aircraft. Once more their activities provoked counter-action and for the second time the Japanese tried to pre-empt the dive-bombers with a sneak attack of their own against their base.

This raid took place between 05.00 and 05.07 on the morning of 12 March 1944. Three Japanese bombers, believed to be Army Type 97 twin-engined machines, came in with shallow dives from 10,000ft down to 7000ft on Kumbhirgram.

They came in from the south and withdrew to west-south-west. The weather was fine, with no cloud and a full moon. The Japanese dropped twelve 30kg, one 50kg high-explosive bomb (HE), and nine 30kg HE bombs, killing six civilians and injuring another eight. One 84 Squadron machine was damaged by a burning camouflage net falling on to it and three aircraft from 110 Squadron received minor damage but all proved repairable. Two *basha* huts containing engine and airframe stores were completely destroyed. The heavy AA-fire engaged the enemy planes, firing 26 rounds which split up the three-plane formation after the bombs had dropped, as these were standing orders. Again, such a tiny raid had little or no effect upon the high rate of the British dive-bombers' sorties which continued unabated.

More dangerous were the hazards of jungle navigation and the unpredictable monsoon weather, steadily gaining in intensity as the months passed. On one typical mission in April the dive-bombers found thick cloud covering all the mountain tops and extending up to 15,000ft. With the main target thus effectively 'weathered out' an alternative was chosen and the dive-bombers accordingly changed course and attacked Paung-byin. There were six Vengeances from 84 Squadron and six from 7 Squadron, all armed with two 500-lb bombs and eight 30-lb incendiaries. The attack itself was successful, but on the homeward leg they flew into bad weather after an overall mission time of 2 hours 15 minutes. Two of 7 Squadron's aircraft never returned at all and crashed somewhere in the lonely, mist-covered mountains.

The treacherous nature of these mountain ranges and the unpredictable weather conditions were shown soon after the Chindit operation began further north. Seventy-eight gliders and 660 Dakota sorties had landed over 9000 men, 1360 pack animals and associated equipment, with the loss by accident of only 121 men in gliders. It was a magnificent achievement but on 24 March fate struck a particularly cruel blow when the American-crewed plane carrying Orde Wingate himself was caught in the same conditions and exploded against the side of a mountain.

This type of danger faced the dive-bomber squadrons constantly. The mountain ranges quickly became cul-de-sacs, with no way over and insufficient room to turn back. Death traps for the unwary. Fuel economy was also a continual worry, as Arthur Gill, the CO of 84 Squadron, relates:

> Having been trained with Wingate we had this problem of having targets much further than other squadrons. Whereas 45 and 110 Squadrons were bombing targets quite near Imphal and were therefore able to get there and back within half-an-hour or so, some of our trips were nearly three hours in duration. We had an emergency rule laid down that if we were short of fuel, if your gauges were down to a certain level by the time you passed over the Imphal plain, you didn't go over the next range of mountains. That would be your 'furthest-out' point. But apart from one or two losses, only a few aircraft whose engines were a bit thirsty ever had problems and were forced to land at one of the emergency airstrips we set up.
>
> A lot depended on how you flew. We, at any rate, climbed carefully. Unlike some other squadrons which would roar off and then get quickly into formation and then roar up to cruising height, we, however, did a much more gentle climb using less power, because you used more fuel on the initial climb than you used on the rest of the flight. So one would climb up steadily over the mountains and then cut back on the throttle to cruise out to the target, keeping as much fuel as possible in your tanks. We'd cruise at perhaps only 180mph, whereas some of the other squadrons would go at over 190mph which drank a lot more fuel.

But no amount of fuel economy could solve the problem of thick cloud over the jungle-clad hills. Not all the heights and locations of the mountains had been reliably charted in the earlier years, simply because the need had not yet arisen for flying over such territory, much less fight an air war over and through it. So the pilots and navigators had to rely equally on their vision and expertise to get them out of tight situations. The extremely turbulent nature of the monsoon clouds also could catch out the less experienced flyers. Even those with local knowledge had sometimes to face the grim fact that, with no way to go around, they had to go through such unpredictable formations, sometimes with dire results. The story of Pilot Officer Gabrielson is a case in point. Arthur Gill recalls:

> The background was that 'B' Flight, 8 Squadron, led by Dick
> Johns, a New Zealand Flight Commander, flew into a very bad
> storm. They initially went right into one of the big cumulus clouds.
> These clouds have upcurrents of 100mph to 150mph and the
> aircraft were just scattered, thrown all over the sky. Surprisingly
> not one of them hit each other, even though they were shot off in all
> directions. Now Gabrielson was in the back of 'U' for Uncle.
> Fortunately he had his parachute clipped on.
>
> The pilot lost control of the aircraft when it was caught in one of
> the upcurrents, and Gabrielson, at that moment turning in his
> swivel seat without being strapped in, was thrown clear of the open
> cockpit. He lost his helmet in the slip-stream, and so could not
> communicate his plight. He dangled half in, half out of the aircraft
> before he could hit the quick-release clip, and parachuted down
> into the jungle behind the Japanese lines. After many adventures,
> which would make a tale of their own, he eventually rejoined his
> unit completely unscathed by his ordeals.

Because it was so difficult for the jungle dive-bomber crews to
know whether their direct hits were having the desired effect it
became common for the Army to let them know by signal just
how effective they were. These signals were known as 'Strawberries' in order to distinguish them from the better known
'Raspberries' which orthodox bombing had hitherto evoked
from their brothers-in-arms. With dive-bombing it proved very
different.

On 8 April 1944, for example, the Vengeance squadrons
carried out a Long Range Penetration Group (LRPG) mission,
a 450-mile flight to Mawlu on the Irrawaddy to dive-bomb
Japanese bunker positions overlooking one of the Chindit
landing strips. On this occasion there was direct radio contact
with the LRPG column and the well-rehearsed smoke indication
technique was put into effect. Despite heavy AA-fire from
Mawlu itself an extremely accurate attack was delivered. Each
of the twelve Vultee aircraft deposited one 500-lb bomb and
one 250-lb GP bomb with an 11-second fuse, and one 500-lb
and one 250-lb with a 0.025-second fuse, into the target. They
were airborne for 2 hours 50 minutes but all returned safely.

Reports later from the 3 Indian Division stated that the enemy bunker positions were all destroyed. A later signal reported that 265 dead Japanese were found in the area.

A similar operation took place on 15 April 1944 against an Army Air Support Command target. Two dozen Vengeances were sent in against large numbers of Japanese troops dug in on a ridge south of Sagolmang, 10 miles north-east of Imphal. This was closer to base and all four squadrons quickly deposited 36,000-lb of bombs along the ridge after 4 Corps reported that the Ghurkas went in with the bayonet immediately after this dive-bombing attack and occupied the whole area with little opposition. Over 450 dead Japanese were counted.

Some of the 'Strawberries' received following these early missions expressed appreciation as follows:

To: 168 Wing 84 Squadron 110 Squadron
From: 221 Group A9M56 2 March 1944

Secret Message from 2 and 3 Vic Force Ops Area. Sincere thanks to all personnel for prompt action and co-operation taken on all demands for support.

To: 168 Wing via 23 ASC
From: Brigade Major 17 Division 17 April 1944

Bombing 300 yards from our own troops on smoke indicator excellent.
Mile 99 Tiddim Road

Phone Message from 23 ASC 23 April 1944

Your bombing this morning TOT 09.40. Ground sources report your bombing a bull's-eye. Bloody good show.

Signal To: 168 Wing
From: Adv HQs 3 Indian Division 23 April 1944

Secret. Commander Special Force congratulates all ranks 84 Squadron on excellent results obtained in bombing targets today.

Phone message. To: Squadron-Leader A. M. Gill
From: Colonel G. S., HQ, 3 Indian Division 23 April 1944

Thanks for the very fine show you put up today; the bombing was excellent.

Signal: To: 84 Squadron
From: 25 ASC A43 27 April 1944

Following from Commander 2 Division. Very many thanks splendid air support today. Bulk of Vengeance on target area.

Signal: To: Engineering Officer 110 Squadron
From: 25 ASC 4 May 1944

General Glover commanding Kohima operations has asked that his appreciation be conveyed to you for air support today, particularly to crews of Vengeance and Hurricanes who operated successfully despite adverse weather over target early this morning. The Vengeances arrived at the right moment and the aircraft kept the Japanese heads down for the rest of the operation.

Each squadron had its particular style and Arthur Gill recalled Dennis Gibbs's 82 Squadron:

A great showman! He impressed me a lot when he first arrived from the Arakan. Suddenly we heard this tremendous noise. Whereas 84 Squadron would return to base very gently and politely, Dennis arrived with his squadron in very tight formation, really packed in close, with four flights stepped down, very low, they couldn't have been flying at more than, say, 300ft. The last and bottom aircraft was almost touching the trees, or so it seemed to us watching and you can imagine the noise from 16 Vengeance engines. He then pulled up and went straight ahead. His other two flights split up and went low down all the way round the back and then they all lined up to land.

Take-offs were the same. As we had been trained to undertake long-range missions with Wingate and so knew about flying further into Burma and making every drop of fuel count, we climbed carefully up. I noticed that 82 would roar off and then quickly get into formation and then roar up to cruising height, whereas we did a much more gentle climb using less power on the flight. So one would climb up steadily over the mountains and then cut back on throttle to cruise out to the target, keeping as much fuel as possible.

Four RAF squadrons equipped with the Vultee Vengeance – Squadrons 45, 82, 84 and 110 (H) – and two Indian Air Force squadrons, too, were forging this plane into a very potent weapon for jungle fighting. Two squadrons worked on the coast along the Arakan front while the other four operated further up into the Irrawaddy valley and all were in continuous demand in much the same way as 84 Squadron. Gradually, however, as the Battle of the Boxes developed into a chase of the remnants of the Japanese divisions back into the hinterland, the Vengeance was replaced by Mosquito aircraft. Number 45 Squadron was the first to convert, while the two Indian units became Spitfire squadrons. Even so in the final days of the Burma conflict these Spitfires were dive-bombing the harassed enemy columns as they fled southward, maintaining the old traditions of the Vengeance to the end. Eventually, by June 1944, the only RAF squadron which remained fighting with the Vultee Vengeance was 84 Squadron. Being the only precision unit on station it was in great demand. As Gill said:

We did bomb the Ya-Na'n bridge several times. Of course they would rebuilt it again. In a case like that we would send over only about six to eight aircraft to destroy a bridge, didn't need more than that. Vital roads as well. Intelligence sources would come back that the Japanese have now occupied such-and-such and they would tell us where they were actually operating. Not jungle targets at this stage of the war so much, this is on the Imphal plain, all paddy-fields and marshland, very, very wet country.

When the monsoons came we found that 12 aircraft would take off, fly all the way to the target and couldn't find it because it would be completely covered with cloud, 'weathered out'. So I said to the AOC, Air Marshal Vincent, could I have a Spitfire, then I, or one of my Flight Commanders, could fly over to the target area and if it was clear, signal back in plain language to come and get them. I said it would save thousands of wasted flying hours. We flog all the way out and all the way back wasting engine hours and fuel. He said 'That sounds all right' and gave me this Spit and we called it 'The Looker'. On one occasion I flew out to the target and ran into these two Japanese fighters and I shot one down. I got a pat on the back with one hand and a good ticking off with the other as they didn't know I was out there. They threatened to take my Spit away if I did it again.

A regular target towards the end of June 1944 was the vital bridges serving as supply and escape routes for the Japanese Army. Many missions were mounted against them. The Elephant bridge north of Tamu was damaged by a 12-plane strike on 19 June. Each of 84 Squadron's aircraft carried two 500-lb and two 250-lb bombs. On 28 June 12 Vengeances, each with a 1500-lb bombload, attacked the Williams bridge, north of Tamu, scoring hits which damaged it. They also strafed the target with 400 rounds. On 28 June the bridge over the Lokcho river, west of Sibong on the Tamu to Palel road, was damaged by near-misses despite poor weather conditions. Gill continued:

On some such specialised strikes we had all bombs fused with 11-second delay. In fact, on the Ya-Na'n bridge which we bombed several times, we would not only drop 11-second delay bombs which would blow the bridge up after we had flown away from it, but we would also drop 12-hour and 24-hour and 36-hour delay bombs. So that as they came back and repaired it and said that was a good job, Boom! But of course it would worry them once this had happened because they couldn't see where the bombs had dropped into the water and so on and would not know when the next one was due to go off.

With the monsoons the cloud stretched from 30,000ft down to ground-level and so finding a target was a problem. But as the cloud lifted in between the storms one could often get to the target, but at a lower level, say at 5000ft, instead of our normal 12,000ft or 13,000ft. So we devised this system of nipping in and out of the cloud, but you hadn't got enough height to peel off and dive vertically because you'd kill yourself. So what we did was introduce this shallow-dive technique of running up alongside the target and doing a gentle turn-off, keeping the target in sight all the way, and diving down at only 45 degrees.

This could never be as accurate as proper dive-bombing which, despite what the 'experts' have since kept on repeating, we *always* carried out at between 85–90 degrees. So it would not be as accurate as that but you had to adjust for conditions and gauge it.

1 US Marine Corps Major Ross ('Rusty') Rowell flew DH-4 aircraft in the mid 1920s in Nicaragua against the Sandinistas. These were the first jungle dive-bombing combat missions

2 A Curtiss P-40 fighter of the famous 'Flying Tigers' who achieved the first strategic victory by dive-bombers in the Far East at the battle of the Salween Gorge in 1942

3 The aircrew of the Japanese navy's Kokutai 2 at Rabaul in 1942 before
their special mission with their short-range Aichi dive-bombers refuelling
behind Allied lines then flying on to the target deep in New Guinea

4 Troops of a Japanese island garrison performing the worshipping ceremony
for the Emperor's birthday on 29 April 1942 in front of an Aichi D3A1
'Val' at an airbase in the Philippines

A Japanese 'Val' dive-bomber on a combat mission against Allied forces in Papua or the Solomons, *c.* September 1942

Ditched and abandoned Aichi D3A1 'Val' on the beach at Table Bay, Papua, in September 1942 after an abortive behind-the-lines dive-bomber mission had gone badly wrong

7 An Australian Vultee Vengeance of No 12 Squadron RAAF in camouflaged revetment; such aircraft carried out the first Australian combat dive-bombing in June 1943 against targets on Selaru Island in the Arafura Sea

8 Australian Vultee Vengeances returning to Nadzab, New Guinea, after another strike at Japanese positions on the north coast of New Guinea in 1944. Note the distinctive white markings of the tail unique to Allied aircraft in this war zone

9 Australian Vultee Vengeance dive-bombers of No 12 Squadron RAAF. Note the large capacious fuselage and internal bomb-bay; the Vengeance was a big aircraft for a dive-bomber but performed very well in that configuration

10 Australian navigator Ron Gabrielson whose extraordinary adventure after baling out over enemy lines in Burma in spring 1944, while serving with No 84 Squadron RAF, typified the hazards of jungle air war

11 Underview of a bomb-bay of an Australian Vultee Vengeance dive-bomber of No 12 Squadron RAAF

12 W/Cdr Arthur Murland Gill of No 84 Squadron RAF used a Spitfire, nicknamed 'The Looker', to carry out reconnaissance sorties ahead of dive-bomber strikes

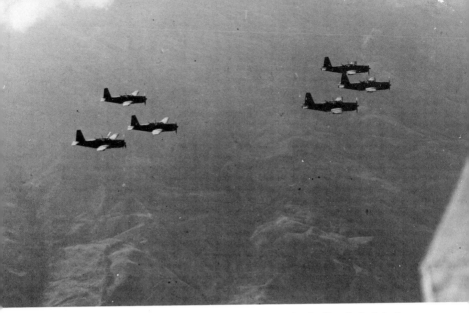

13 A full wing strike against a Japanese-held village in the Imphal plain is
    led over frontier mountain ranges by No 84 Squadron RAF, May 1944

14 The silhouette of a Vultee Vengeance over the Burmese jungle gives an
    indication of the difficulty of locating and destroying targets in such terrain

15 The US Navy Construction Battalions ('Seebees') at work. The ability
of these versatile engineers to transform dense jungle into usable airstrips
within days of a landing did much to maintain the momentum of the island-
hopping campaign through the Solomons chain towards Rabaul

16 SBD5 Dauntless dive-bombers of No 25 Squadron RNZAF taxiing along
one of the temporary airstrips (jointed metal strips bolted together) on
Bougainville island

17 'Today's target is . . .':
typical briefing session for a
US Marine Corps dive-
bomber unit in the Pacific

18 Marine Corps dive-bombers attack ammunition dumps and flak batteries
along the edges of the already well-cratered Bougainville airfields

19 Mission accomplished: another dive-bomber target obliterated, a Marine
Corps SBD5 heads back to base crossing the densely vegetated mountain
ranges of New Britain

20 S/Ldr T. J. MacLean de Lange (r) who led No 25 Squadron RNZAF during the Bougainville campaign with such success

21 Another pasting for Rabaul: New Zealand Dauntless flights lead another mass strike against the Japanese base in 1944

22 Dauntless over New Britain: a SBD5 of No 25 Squadron RNZAF flies low over a Japanese-held area searching out fresh targets during 1944

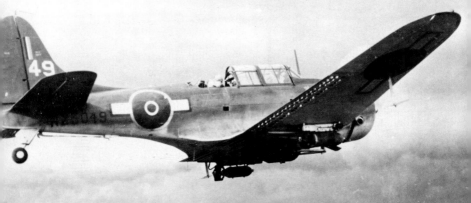

23 The Japanese Yokosuka D4Y, 'Judy', operating mainly from jungle and island airbases, scored some of the most devastating dive-bombing hits on carriers of the US Task Forces

24 Japanese navy ground crew working on a Yokosuka D4Y, 'Judy', at a forward base in the Philippines area in 1944 in readiness to strike back at the approaching American fleet

25 A gaggle of Curtiss SB-2C Helldivers returns to Task Force 58 after missions over Saipan in late 1944

26 The distinctive pose of a Curtiss SB-2C Helldiver with bomb-doors open. The crutch which swung the bombs out and down is retracted – or obliterated by an over-zealous censor – but unit markings are clearly visible as the 1000-lb bomb plummets towards the target

27 The Air Commando units
of the USAAF were set up
in north Assam and other
A-36 Invader dive-bombers
and P-51 Mustang fighter-
bombers were deployed in
support of General
Stilwell's forces and Brig-
General Frank D. Merrill's
Marauders operating deep
in the jungle

28 A Mustang pilot of the
composite Chinese/
American wing examines
flak damage to his P-51
Mustang after a successful
dive-bomber mission over
the Chinese/Burmese
border area

29 Indo-China, 1954: a French patrol moves into a village near Dien Bien Phu to 'mop up' in the wake of a dive-bombing attack. Such scenes were familiar in jungle warfare, with a determined enemy prepared to die in last-ditch ambushes regardless of losses

30 French navy Helldivers, commanded by Lieutenant de Vaisseau H. de Lestapis, on patrol over the Tonkin delta in 1954

31 Helldivers of the French navy's 3 Flotille d'Assault lined up at Bach Mai airbase near Hanoi in April 1954 when they were being operated against Vietminh forces in Indo-China

32 Scourge of jungle infantrymen: a target's-eye view of a Douglas Dauntless with distinctive 'cheese-grater' dive-brakes lowered

The hazards of low-level attack were made evident in one such raid conducted on 5 July. Gill led a strike of 12 Vengeances against stores and troops at Le–U. The attacks were made utilising the shallow-dive method, in flights of three. The target was an ammunition dump and was strongly defended by AA-fire, 20mm and 37mm being encountered, but the damage came not from this but from the Vengeance's own success. The bombs were on target and resulted immediately in a huge explosion, due probably to a landmine or ammunition blowing up. The Vengeance of Sergeant Natrass, Gill's No 3, was caught directly in this upblast and very severely damaged. It was nursed back to base and the crew, though shaken, were not badly injured. The new tactic was initiated against a bridge target on 29 June when Gill led three Vengeances carrying 500-lb 11-second delay bombs against the Ya-Na'n bridge. Direct hits were scored, the bridge was breached in two places and the central span collapsed.

The final attack by 84 Squadron, indeed the final, historic, combat mission flown by the Vultee Vengeance, took place on 16 July 1944. Arthur Gill flew a Vengeance III (FB–981), with Flight Lieutenant Blackburn as navigator. Twelve Vengeances flew against the ammunition dumps at Le–U to carry out a low-level attack; 10/10th cloud persisted for most of the flight and covered the mountains in a grim pall, but they found their target and the strike was put in. 'Accurate bombing', Gill noted in his Log. An overall mission time was recorded of two hours and five minutes.

That was the swan-song of the Vengeance in the RAF's combat line for, like its Australian and Indian counterparts, its success failed to save it. By 4 August Arthur Gill was on the Afghan Frontier overflying the famous old Chaman Fort and three days later he helped in the search for 82 Squadron's missing aircraft. Number 84 Squadron was scheduled to convert to Mosquitos but Gill's own last flight in the Vengeance took place on 25 September 1944. He was posted home and flew FB981 from Samungli, Quetta, to Lahore, escorted for part of the way by a flight of Vengeances from the unit which he had first preserved, then led so well.

Like so much of the work of General Slim's 'Forgotten Army' in that grim campaign in Burma, little is now remembered of the achievements of the Vengeance Wings in the jungle fighting. Yet even less is known about the dedicated work of a group of American dive-bombers, the 'Secret Squadrons', during the same period.

6
The Secret Squadrons

While the principal dive-bomber operations along the Indo-Burmese border during 1943–4 had been conducted by the Vultee Vengeance of the RAF and the Indian Air Force, further north the United States Army Air Force had continued the traditions established by Chennault's valiant P–40 units. Both 51 and 80 Fighter Groups, equipped also with the P–40, had conducted dive-bombing missions from bases in Assam. Their targets were Japanese airfields, ground forces and positions threatening the vital air route over 'The Hump' which was now used as an aerial supply line to replace the Japanese-controlled Burma Road. Thus the tradition of the P–40 as a dive-bomber was continued with 500-lb bomb loads being delivered against targets at the eastern end of the route in co-operation with the American and Chinese forces holding these remote areas.

The main battle developed when the Japanese 55 Division launched its attack in three thrusts hoping to cut off and encircle 7 Indian Division. The victorious Japanese would then advance from Arakan into India towards Chittagong, and this would be coupled with a general uprising in Bengal itself. This in turn would herald the main Japanese thrust of 100,000 men which was to crash through the Manipur Valley and smash open the very centre of the Allied front defending the subcontinent.

Meanwhile the British 14 Army, having been slowly and painfully built up in readiness and learning from the two previous abortive attacks, had laid their own offensive plans against the ending of the monsoon season. They hoped to attack along the coast as far as the Naf River to clear the vital lifeline of the Maungdaw-Buthidaung road and much of the Mayu peninsula. While a diversion was made by 81 West African

Division down the Kaladan Valley, the main British thrusts were to be delivered by 7 Indian Division to take Buthidaung and cut off Letwedet, while 5 Indian Division had as its objectives the strategic towns of Maungdaw and Razabil.

The new Japanese offensive was launched on 4 February 1944 into what developed into the third Arakan campaign. But it was their 'U-Operation', designed to start in March, which led to the main land battles of the Burma war and the heavy involvement of the 'Secret Squadrons' of American dive-bombers. This ambitious plan had as its objectives the seizure of the 'Hump' airfields, thus stifling the last available supply route for Chiang Kai-shek's forces and the American 14 Air Force in China, to cut also the lifeline of General Stilwell's operation out of Ledo by taking the Bengal-Assam railway at Dimapur, to wipe out the British IV Corps, and to start the final drive on Delhi itself.

General Wingate's airborne operation, with the aim of doing a similar job behind the Japanese lines, had anticipated, but did not delay, the main Japanese attack. He relied heavily on accurate air support, not just from the British and Indian Vengeance squadrons but from American dive-bombers.

By the time these events began to take shape, the elderly American makeshift P–40 dive-bombers had been replaced along this front by a much more efficient weapon, the North American A–36A Invader. This aircraft had developed in the United States out of the original North American P–51 Mustang fighter aircraft which had been designed for the RAF but which the USAAF had at first largely ignored. Some 500 P–51s were designed to be equipped with dive brakes and underwing bomb racks specifically in order to operate as dive-bombers in close support. First flown in September 1942 the Apache, as it was initially dubbed, was also armed with six 0.5in. machine-guns and powered by a 1325-hp Allison engine. This resulted in a very fast and man-oeuvrable single-seater dive-bomber. The first units went to North Africa and served in the Sicilian and Italian campaigns, but the overriding need for such an aircraft led to the assigning of 311 Fighter Bomber Group to the northern Burma front.

Because supplies of the Invader, as the A–36 subsequently became more generally known, were limited, it was supplemented by P–51A Mustangs. These were also adapted from fighters by the addition of bomb racks which were to prove capable of carrying 1000-lb bombs (although in theory 500lb was the maximum recommended load) or drop tanks. It had a 1200-hp engine and only four 0.5in. machine-guns but could also carry long-range drop fuel tanks. Aircraft would carry a drop tank under one wing and a 500-lb bomb under the other for long-range pre-emptive strikes against Japanese airfields. A special close-support group was set up to help support Orde Wingate's operations and this unit, 1 Air Commando Group commanded by Colonel Philip Cochran, worked operationally under 3 Tactical Air Force and Air Marshal Baldwin who, like Arthur Gill of 84 Squadron, planned the dive-bomber requirements directly with Wingate himself. They reached the front in January 1944, and became operational the following month when it was the first Mustang unit to dive-bomb with 1000-lb bombs. These P–51s were identified by the special markings of five diagonal white stripes painted across the rear fuselage behind the cockpit, the SEAC (South-East Asia Command) version of the better known 'Invasion' stripes of D-Day and after in Europe. Basic operational airfields for them were hacked out of the jungle of north-central Burma by American combat engineers.

Another innovation introduced by this Group was the fitting of American 'bazooka'-type rocket-launching tubes in clusters of three under each wing. Great care had to be taken in their use, however, as the turbulence set up by the rockets' discharge affected the pivot tube pressure which in turn resulted in a variation of some 20mph in the Indicated Air Speed shown. This could result in some tricky landings, if it was believed. However, the use of such weapons was such that fitting the tubes became general practice for all Mustang units. The Air Commando was very active between February and May 1944 and rendered invaluable assistance during both the initial Chindit landings and the Japanese counter-attacks at Kohima and Imphal. On its withdrawal it was replaced by 2 Air

Commando Group which carried on flying the P–51D Mustang in the close-support role.

But it is the work of the true dive-bomber group that is worthy of more detailed attention. 311 Bombardment Group (Light) originated with General Order 15 issued on 2 March 1942 by HQ 2 Air Force. It was set up at Will Rogers Field in Oklahoma and comprised four Bombardment squadrons: 382, 383, 384 and 385. In July it moved to Savannah and, in October, to Waycross, also in Georgia. With General 'Hap' Arnold's requirement to provide the US Army with dive-bomber units as a priority the designation was changed to 311 Bombardment Group (Dive) on 1 July of the same year. Its first Commanding Officer was Lieutenant-Colonel John R. Kelly who was relieved by Lieutenant-Colonel Harry R. Melton, jnr, in December, and he in turn from 25 November 1943 by Lieutenant-Colonel Charles G. Chandler, jnr, the former Executive Officer.

Originally 311 Bombardment Group was to have been a Vengeance V–72 unit, like its British and Indian counterparts in Burma at this time, but this was changed after several months' training by the arrival of the new, fast, single-seater A–36A and in December 1942 all the Vultees were replaced by Invaders, 'much to the pleasure and satisfaction of both pilots and ground personnel'. The only individuals who regretted the change were the gunners who immediately became redundant and were shipped out of the Group. Training continued with the new aircraft, the A–36As being supplemented by P–51As from June 1943. Combat crews were trained with both types, the P–51A being described as 'a higher altitude ship, a later model of the A–36, with only minor differences'. It was added that: 'This plane is used principally as a fighter plane but is easily adapted to bomber strategy and may carry a maximum load of 1000 lb carried on exterior bomb racks'. The unit was again re-designated on 30 September 1943 as 311 Fighter Bomber Group with three squadrons – 528, 529 and 530 – the first equipped with about two dozen A–36A Invaders, while the latter was a P–51A Mustang squadron.

The Group carried out detailed training and went on man-oeuvres with ground troops at Pope Field, North Carolina, early in 1943. When all stages of the OTU training had been completed, 311 Group was assigned to the China-Burma-India (CBI) Combat Theatre and departed on 18 July 1943, each squadron leaving at a different hour and the pilots flying their individually assigned planes from Waycross to Camp Stoneman, Alameda, California. They arrived there by 24 July, and some of the planes were crated and all loaded in readiness to be shipped across the Pacific to India, via Australia to Karachi.

The men of the group themselves went aboard the US Army Transport *Brazil* which sailed from San Francisco on 31 July, reaching Bombay on 10 September 1943 after an uneventful voyage via Hobart, Tasmania, and Fremantle. Here they were taken by train to Nawadih where they remained until 10 October when they were sent by train to their combat airfields in northern Assam. When the crew chiefs arrived in Bombay they were flown immediately to Karachi to prepare the planes for flying, each pilot being flown out in order personally to fly his own aircraft to its new base. 528 Squadron ultimately moved into Sookerating with its A–36s; 529 Squadron and 530 Squadron, both with P–51s, to Dinjan and Mohanbari respectively.

The Group's first assignment was to act in direct defence of the Brahmaputra Valley. This included offensive missions against enemy troop and supply concentrations in northern Burma in readiness for General Stilwell's planned offensive. The very first combat mission was carried out on 16 October 1943 when eight Invaders dive-bombed and strafed the town of Sumprabum in northern Burma with good effect and without loss.

Further dive-bombing missions followed on an almost daily basis. The targets were located either by photo-reconnaissance, which confirmed intelligence gathering, or at ground level. The A–36s successfully attacked Japanese targets at the villages of Kamaing, Mogaung, Pamati, Taipha Ga, Waingmaw, Myitkyina, Taro, Lonkin, Walawbum, Naba and Manywet. In their own element now, the dive-bombers scored valuable hits.

Because of their potential as both fighters and dive-bombers the Invaders and the Mustangs were also pressed into service as escorts for the C–47 Dakota transport planes of 1 and 2 Troop Carrier Squadrons on the 'Hump' route over the Fort Hertz valley, and for bombing raids on the Rangoon area by Mitchell and Liberator bombers of both 7 and 490 Bomber Groups. They also conducted their own long-range fighter intruder sorties over Japanese fighter bases. For this reason one squadron of P–51As was moved to Kurmitola in India. There were never more than 20 P–51As to protect up to 50 bombers, however, and at a distance of up to 670 miles. A sharp lesson was soon learnt because the Japanese 'Haps' and 'Oscar' fighters proved far more manoeuvrable and agile, and, in particular, the Japanese aces of 64 Sentai, based at Mingaladon and Bhamo, found the Americans inexperienced and inflicted several losses on the Group, including the Commanding Officer, Colonel Harry R. Melton. In November he was forced to bale out during a combat mêlée in which three other Mustangs were lost when escorting Liberator bombers to Insein, making eight American losses in all.

More successful were the close-support operations carried out in the Hukawng Valley. These were intended to soften up the Japanese positions in readiness for the attack southward by the Chinese 22 and 38 Divisions. Supply parachuting by Dakotas was also carried out and the P–51s provided top cover and also strafed the drop zone area to nullify enemy anti-aircraft fire as the transports came in low for the food drops. Fighter interceptions had to be conducted also over the Brahmaputra Valley and the Digbol Refinery when the enemy struck back with air attacks of their own.

At the end of 1943, 311 Group, under the command of Lieutenant-Colonel Charles G. Chandler, had Captain George W. Alexander as Commanding Officer of 528 Squadron, Major Augustus E. Rickenbaker and Captain Sidney M. Newcomb, the Commanding Officers respectively of 529 and 530 squadrons. Their role was defined by a letter dated 27 December 1943:

The primary mission of 311 Fighter Bomber Group is to furnish air support to the ground forces in the area. In addition to direct support of the ground forces they will be utilized against enemy lines of communications, supply dumps and concentrations within their operating range.

Dinjan was the HQ field, and the only Japanese activity directed against it had been a raid of 20-plus Japanese bombers on 13 December 1943 which surprisingly inflicted no damage at all. While 530 Squadron was detached on bomber escort missions the other two squadrons conducted 98 bombing and strafing missions. Up to the end of January 1944, in fact, some 104 bombing, strafing and escort missions had been flown and 113 tons of bombs dropped. Their operations ranged over a wide area from the Dalu Valley from Maingkwan in the west and north, to Mohuyinin in the south and Ningchangyong and Fort Hertz valley in the east. With some 150 officers and 784 enlisted men on their strength 311 Group exerted an influence on the enemy dispositions far in excess of their numbers.

The softening-up of the enemy in the Upper Hukawng Valley continued to be the premier mission for the Invaders during February and March 1944, however. The A–36s were able to use their unique accuracy to make telling strikes on such targets as bivouac areas, ammunition dumps, troop concentrations, gun emplacements, warehouses, fortified villages and supply dumps as and when they were positively identified. Nor were the back area targets ignored with the American dive-bombers hitting at lines of supply and communication further south, the bombing of road and rail bridges as always being the most effective means of delaying enemy build-ups, while the strafing of trucks and railway locomotives and trucks caused the Japanese maximum disruption for the minimum of effort. So effective had this become that daylight operations by such units had almost ceased by the end of March.

As in other jungle dive-bomber units, the outstanding results of sortie ratios and direct hits could be achieved only by the dedication of the ground team, the backroom boys sweltering on the primitive airstrips miles from their main stores, but somehow keeping the A–36As and P–51s airborne and active. During March 1944, for example, the average percentage of assigned airplanes actually in commission, despite all the adverse conditions, was 98 per cent for 530 Squadron, 94.2 per cent for 529 Squadron, and 93.8 per cent for 528 Squadron. The latter unit, of course, had more planes on its strength than the combined total of the other two. During the whole of that month's operations serviceability for the Group never fell below 90 per cent. One squadron indeed had 100 per cent of its assigned aircraft in commision for twenty days during the month and the total number of 100-per-cent days for all three squadrons was 30. These were magnificent achievements, especially considering that the Group flew more combat sorties in March 1944 than any other month since leaving the United States, and that practically all the aircraft and their engines had passed the 'life expectancy' of equipment in combat conditions.

As the Chinese pressed forward, they had the American unit 'Merrill's Marauders' as their spearhead. Officially designated '5307 Composite Volunteers', Merrill's Marauders, commanded by Brigadier Frank D. Merrill, were the US equivalent of the Chindits, fighting behind enemy lines. More conventional dive-bomber targets presented themselves as the Japanese made stands to halt them. As with the German Stuka and British Vengeance squadrons, the effectiveness of the support the A–36s were able to provide depended on close liaison with the troops on the ground. Here again 311 Group rotated Air Force officers to work with the actual Marauder battalions in the jungle to co-ordinate strikes via ground-to-air radio links. By the end of the month regular dive-bombing hits were being made by the A–36s within fifty yards of the forward troops at their own direction.

After their initial over-enthusiasm in the fighter role the Group quickly settled down to its proper role, and the trend in tactical operations towards more and more close support continued during April. This was given further impetus by most of the missions of this nature being made in support of Stilwell's and Merrill's forces.

The actual aircraft strength of the Group during this month was as follows:

Squadron	Aircraft Type		1 April	30 April
528	A–36A		24	21
	P–51A1		–	5
	P–51A5		–	2
		Total	24	28
529	P–51A1		5	–
	P–51A5		1	–
	P–51A10		5	–
	P–51B7		–	8
	P–51B10		–	10
		Total	11	18
530	P–51A1		6	13
	P–51A5		–	1
	P–51A10		5	11
		Total	11	25

This type of action was perfected, with the same principles being applied to operations that developed during April and May in support of Sino-American ground forces. To facilitate this, one squadron of Invaders was moved up in May to Tingkawk Sakan in Burma. From here they flew dive-bombing missions not only in direct support of Merrill's troops as they approached Myitkyina but also to aid British forces around Mogaung. On 29 May 1944 no less than 79 sorties were flown in support of ground troops while, in addition, the same day saw 311 Group fly eight patrol sorties in the Myitkyina area, eight more in a dive-bombing and strafing mission against Bhano 2 airstrip, and four top-cover fighter missions by P–51As for B–25 bomber attacks on Sahmaw. A grand total in one day of 99 sorties.

Also in May another squadron was sent south to Dohazari in India for a four-day period during which they flew sweeps over enemy airfields in central and southern Burma from where the

Japanese were mounting heavy air raids in support of their besieging troops at Myitkyina and Imphal. This time the Americans suffered no losses and made several claims of enemy aircraft destroyed. In the north the assault on Mogaung by the Chindits under Wingate's successor, Major-General 'Joe' Lentaigne, was also given dive-bomber back-up. As the official account related, 'The clockwork precision of ground-to-air support being furnished the Chinese-American troops to the north worked just as smoothly with the British-Indian troops driving up from the south.'

Close-support missions continued in both the Mogaung and Myitkyina areas on the Irrawaddy river throughout June and July. At the same time the Group's HQ moved up to Tingkawk Sakan to enhance co-operation between the dive-bombers and the front-line soldiers.

The seizure of Myitkyina airfield was achieved by a special force from Merrill's Marauders codenamed Galahad. This group made a wide sweep from Stilwell's main force driving south and surprised the Japanese who had established there the main supply base for their forces north of Mandalay and constructed an all-weather airfield from which their fighters could menace the 'Hump' route. Now, much in the manner of Henderson Field on Gaudalcanal, the Americans made good use of the Japanese engineers' work.

Within an hour of the airfield falling to Galahad Force, Dakota transports were landing there, to be followed by gliders with more substantial equipment including 12 40mm Bofors AA-guns and British Chindits to reinforce the advance. The audaciousness of such moves is best illustrated by the fact that, although the airfield was in Allied hands, the town of Myitkyina itself was still strongly fortified and held by Japanese forces. Eventually, and even though the siege of Imphal required equal attention from the air forces, a whole Division of Allied troops was flown into Myitkyina. Among the earliest requirements to be based there were, naturally, the close-support dive-bombers. The arrival of 311 Group was one of the decisive moments of the battle.

Like the US Marine dive-bomber crews on Guadalcanal and

the New Zealand crews on Bougainville, the American dive-bomber pilots were operating at this time under the very noses of the enemy. The Official History relates:

> American fighter and dive-bomber squadrons were immediately based on the airfield and, despite the lack of warning of enemy raids – the field was not more, at times, than 1000 yards from the enemy – the presence of the aircraft proved well worth the risk. Proximity to the battlefront meant that they could pack a high rate of sorties into each flying day and also that the Army could see a target being bombed sometimes less than half an hour after requesting action. One pilot accomplished the record of the field by taking off, bombing and returning to base all within ten minutes.

Such fighting continued for 11 weeks as the Japanese clung tenaciously to the town itself and, by the end of that period, take-offs and landings at the airfield were being made at the rate of one a minute. Meanwhile much the same story was unfolding at the other major Japanese supply town of Mogaung which had been taken by the Chindits. This time the American dive-bombers were directed on to their targets by RAF liaison officers dropped with the Chindits, a notable piece of Allied co-operation in all fields.

To assist in this vital work a series of observation posts was set up all around the town and manned RAF personnel under Squadron-Leader Robert Thompson. These were usually RAF flying officers 'resting' between operational tours and was undertaken at some risk as the enemy reacted to their efficiency with determined efforts to wipe them out by artillery bombardment. Each post was directly linked to the others by telephone and could call in accurate and precision dive-bomber attacks on to enemy gun emplacements and deep bunkers right in front of Brigadier Mike Calvert's Chindit troops on the ground.

The outstanding accuracy of the dive-bombers that resulted was emphasised by Brigadier Calvert who sent the following signal to 'Joe' Lentaigne: 'This Brigade could not have captured Mogaung without the assistance of direct air support. The results they accomplished were accurate and decisive.'

The bazooka-armed P–51As featured more and more in those operations and squadrons equipped to give close support to the 14th Army formations who were working their way back south during August along the railway route from Mogaung. That same month saw the historic deployment of 311 Group in the Salween River area. Since those desperate days of 1942 the single-seater fighter dive-bomber had come full circle, but now it was the Japanese who had their backs to the wall and the US dive-bomber pilots who were pressing their advantage home. Japanese troops, dug in around the towns of Tengchung and Lungling, were blasted from their trenches by precise dive-bombing with napalm.

By 5 July the Group had its headquarters as well as 529 Squadron at Dinjan in India; 528 Squadron at Tingkawk Sakan in Burma; and 530 Squadron at Mohanbari in India, with an advanced echelon at Warazup, Burma. The respective Battle Records for each squadron at this date were as follows:

	528	529	530
Bombing and strafing sorties	612	14	–
Escort sorties	22	70	8
Patrol sorties	97	12	–
Combat missions	222	14	1
Combat hours flown	898	5	20
Air miles flown	179,700	41,700	4000
Rounds of ammunition fired	275,121	1,945	–
Gasoline consumed (US gallons)	56,364	26,356	14,100

During August, and up to the end of September, all the surviving A–36s were being replaced by the new P–51Bs, the first three of which had been collected for evaluation from Bangalore in January. It featured a four-bladed propeller and a liquid-cooled Rolls-Royce Merlin engine built by Packard which gave superior performance at higher altitudes; but this in itself brought little slackening in effort as the Group was assigned now to General Chennault's 14 Air Force, and moved over the 'Hump' into China proper. In the period between October 1943 and the end of November 1944, 311 Group had claimed to have destroyed 75 Japanese aircraft, probably destroyed 26 more and damaged 50 in the air, with a further one destroyed and seven damaged on the ground. In the same period they lost 19 of their own.

The Invaders and Mustangs flew over 11,000 combat sorties for more than 23,000 hours of combat flying and 4,700,000 air miles. During that period the US dive-bombers planted more than 2200 tons of bombs on target and expended more than 270,0000 rounds of 0.5in. machine-gun ammunition in strafing runs. It is an enviable record in close-support flying.

The battle of the Salween Gorge (see Ch. 2) had been the greatest dive-bombing triumph of the American Volunteer Group, but it had not marked the end of their efforts in this field. One man in particular, the former Navy torpedo and dive-bomber pilot David 'Tex' Hill, epitomised the spirit of the Group in its last few weeks of existence, and beyond. When the metamorphosis of the AVG into the China Air Task Force (CATF) had taken place on 4 July 1942, 'Tex' Hill had been one of the few to stay on with Chennault and continue the fight. He had no great love for the army but he stayed because, in his own words, 'somebody has to finish this dirty job'.

And so he had kept up the fight. What was not generally known, as he led his flight in the new 23 Fighter Group during the rest of that critical summer of 1942, was that Tex flew with acute malaria. Yet his exploits had been the very stuff of legend.

Initially, the new group had been led by Colonel Robert L. Scott, jnr, from 19 July and it had only twenty flyable aircraft out of a total of 51 Tomahawks and 20 Kittyhawks. These old faithfuls remained their main equipment for another year's hard combat, for not until 1944 did the first Mustangs (P–51A) appear.

Although the battle of Salween Gorge had brought much-needed relief the crisis in China had continued. The Japanese retaliated with heavy and continual night air attacks from July

28 onward against the new force's main base at Hengyang. Despite the base being heavily hit and the crews kept awake, it was Tex Hill who led a dive-bomber strike from that strip the following morning to attack Canton, only being turned back by bad weather, not the enemy. As the raids continued it was Tex who flew a solo night dive-bombing mission against Hankow, the most heavily defended Japanese air base in China at that time, in order to give the rest of the CATF's crews a night's rest.

He later carried out a pinpoint dive-bomber attack on a Japanese gunboat at Kiukiang and sank it, thus avenging the *Panay*, despite the fact of being so ill from malaria that, on return to base, he could hardly climb out of his cockpit. For this he was awarded his second American DFC. He already had been given the British and American medals for his earlier work.

At this time the Japanese flew in their own dive-bombers to Kengtung airstrip on the lower Salween, presumably in order to pay the CATF back in kind and provide their troops with close air support, but they never had the chance to show what they could do for, in a brilliant pre-emptive strike by the CATF to forestall this ploy, eleven of the Japanese aircraft were burnt on the ground and the twelfth was shot down as it attempted to take off.

The American dive-bombers had then ranged further and further afield. In October 1942, for example, all the suitable Kittyhawks had been loaded with 500-lb bombs to attack enemy shipping in Victoria harbour, Hong Kong. They claimed the sinking of a tanker and several freighters. This audacious assault was defended by Zero fighters but, despite this, only one P-40 fell to them. This was the aircraft of Captain P. B. O'Connell. In fact it was his bomb that had sunk the tanker for, ignoring the two Zero fighters which were hard on his tail, he continued to press home his attack. Within a few seconds of his bomb hitting the tanker and blowing up, O'Connell's aircraft also exploded and disintegrated into the harbour.

In a similarly brave manner had Major Richardson led a volunteer night mission of P-40s to dive-bomb Hankow docks in the face of the heaviest flak and searchlight defences in China.

Using unsuitable fighter aircraft as dive-bombers both the American Volunteer Group and the China Air Task Force did wonders with what they had. Losses were inevitable but, considering the odds against them – and the age of the aircraft and the difficulties of merely operating at all – the casualty rate was low. Nor did the introduction of dive-bombing sorties greatly increase it over the normal interceptor losses. It is true that some pilots were killed carrying out dive-bomber missions while others like Tex Hill seemed to lead charmed lives. Notable among those lost was Bob Little, a former Army pilot.

Bob Little's last mission took place on 22 May 1942. In company with Joe Tosbert and Charley Sawyer, he conducted a dive-bombing attack on Japanese gun emplacements near to Paoshan, again close to the Salween. It called for a most deliberate approach and the lowest possible release height. The Kittyhawks pressed on down in steep dives to within 1000ft before letting go their 30-lb bombs. Heavy flak hosed up to meet them and the right wing of Little's machine was knocked off by direct hits. As his machine carried on straight in he stood no chance, yet he was one of only eight pilots killed in action between 18 December 1941 and 4 July 1942.

The China Air Task Force was only a temporary unit, and it was itself replaced in 1943 by 14 Air Force. The Americans were more readily inclined at this period to invest equipment rather than manpower in Chennault's force. Thus came about the Chinese-American Composite Wing (CACW). Originally the idea was that the CACW should start off as a mixed force and that gradually the American pilots and ground crews would be replaced by Chinese until only the aircraft remained American. This in fact did not occur. From the time of its formation in November 1943, the American personnel complement increased and the CACW remained a mixed force for the whole of its 21-month existence.

The strength of the CACW, under Colonel Winslow Morse, was two fighter groups: 3 Group (Lieutenant-Colonel T. Alan Bennett) and 5 Group (Lieutenant-Colonel Frank Rouse), and 1 Bomb Group. Each comprised four squadrons apiece. 3 Group assimilated the old Tomahawks and added some of the new P–40Ks from 57 Fighter Group in North Africa. 5 Group formed in Florida with P40–Ns and then shipped out via India, being based initially at Kweilin. Imitating 1 Air Commando's Mustangs in Burma, many of the P–40s were fitted with bazooka-style rocket launchers for ground attack at Chanyi. They were ready for their first missions in May 1944, when the Allies were again on the defensive as the Japanese ICHIGO offensive began to roll south to Hankow down along the Siang river into Indo-China, destroying the 14 Air Force bases in eastern China as they went.

All types of mission occupied the squadrons at this period. Number 32 Fighter Squadron (Captain Bill Turner) had its rocket tubes fitted at Hanchung and carried out its first attacks with these weapons on 22 May against Japanese armoured cars, tanks and cavalry at Loyang on the Yellow River rail link to Hsian. They landed at this base after the attack but just what it meant to be under Chinese command was made apparent to them here when the airfield's commanding officer refused to fuel their aircraft because he had not been allowed to pick the mission! Nothing daunted, 32 Fighter Squadron was airborne the following day and conducted a spirited dive-bombing and rocket attack at Yuncheng.

Pushed back all along the line, the hard-pressed units welcomed the arrival of the P–51s which they utilised in a dive-bombing role also as they began again to probe back to the east. On 7 March 1945, 7 Fighter Squadron, led by Major Tom Reynolds, made a dive-bomber attack against Nanking. Intercepted by Tojo fighters they changed role and shot down three of their attackers without loss to themselves.

Ironically, the last recorded 'kills' registered by the Chinese/American Composite Wing were of Japanese dive-bombers. Four 'Vals' were found over Suchow airfield on 21 May 1945 by Captain Bob Ferguson and Lieutenant Leo Bugner of 32 Fighter Squadron, and each shot down two of them. Thus ended the long American participation in the air war in China, a hidden story but all the more an astonishing and impressive one.

7
New Zealand's Special Squadron

By the spring of 1944 Allied dive-bomber squadrons were playing a major role in pushing back the great arc of Japanese conquest, known by them and to their unwilling new subjects as the 'South-East Asia Co-Prosperity Zone'. At the extreme western end of the battle line, in Burma and China, it was the British, American and Indian squadrons who had first held the line and then started the advance. In the southern centre it had been the Australian Vengeance Wing which had held up the standard first planted by their brothers in makeshift Boomerang, Wirraway and Kittyhawk squadrons in Papua and New Guinea. At the eastern end of the front, in the long Solomon Islands chain, steady progress was also being made toward reducing the Japanese fortress of Rabaul and in this it was the Douglas Dauntless squadrons of the United States Marine Corps which predominated, from Guadalcanal onwards. But even here the Commonwealth air forces were playing their part, a vital part, in maintaining the dive-bomber pressure. It was during the next great step forward up the bitterly contested island route that one unique but almost forgotten Allied dive-bomber unit found its finest hours.

Number 25 Dive-Bomber Squadron, as its first and only commanding officer Air Commodore T. J. MacLean de Lange told me, 'was the only squadron of its kind in the RNZAF'. But if it was special its achievements in its short life were also second to none in that service.

As part of General Douglas MacArthur's ELKTON offensive against Rabaul it was envisaged that the Allies would advance in two prongs, one up through the northern Solomon Islands from Guadalcanal, the other along the coast of New Guinea to Wewak and the Admiralty Islands. McArthur had called for at least 1800 aircraft to support the 21 divisions he needed to achieve this objective. As part of the South Pacific prong of this grandiose offensive the US Navy, 13 US Army Air Force and the RNZAF would play their part. Later it was decided merely to neutralise and by-pass Rabaul itself, but to do this air bases would still need to be established within range of the many Japanese airfields there.

On 1 November 1943 the US Marines put 3 Division ashore at Empress Augusta Bay, halfway up the western coast of Bougainville, the largest island of the Solomon group, which was garrisoned by a large Japanese force, estimated to be 46,000 soldiers plus 20,000 navy personnel. The Japanese commander, Lieutenant-General Kenda, had expected the attack to be made around Buin in the south of the island and thus the Marines were able to establish their bridgehead easily, but their toe-hold remained small and precarious. This was, however, suitable enough for their purpose which was to construct fighter airfields in the Torokina area in order to support their bombing offensive in neutralising Rabaul. For a short time then there was an uneasy stalemate, with the bulk of the island still in Japanese hands and a counter-attack being organised by the largely still intact Japanese 6 Division.

The RNZAF had taken delivery of nine SBD-3* dive-bombers on extended loan from the US Marine Corps Air Group 14 (MAG-14), which itself was already based on Seagrove, in July 1943. These aircraft were assigned serial numbers NZ5001 to NZ5009 and were used to form the first of the planned RNZAF dive-bomber squadrons in order to comply with the requirements of the ELKTON plan. The unit concerned was 25 Squadron which had been formed at Seagrove, near Auckland, on 31 August 1943. The squadron was due to move over to Waipapakauri the following month and be brought up to full strength later. This plan was never carried out and

---

*SBD: The designation derives from 'Scouting Bombing Dive'. Her nickname was 'Slow But Deadly'.

proved to be a curse because the unit remained in limbo and was regarded for most of the difficult forming-up period, and indeed beyond that, as merely a detached flight. Thus none of the basic essentials, from office furniture to supplies, were easily available. Despite such an inauspicious beginning the squadron, thrown on its own resources and fortitude to a far greater extent than usual, applied itself with dedication which led to a fierce pride in its own independence.

The first nine aircraft were signed for, on behalf of the squadron, by a sergeant from the Whenuapai base. An equipment officer, Flying Officer Barket, was also loaned from Onerahi and he obtained basic supplies from these. Maintenance was a nightmare problem, for obviously the US Marines did not wish to part with their best aircraft. Although 1 Repair Depot at Hamilton supplied back-up, and the Marines themselves chipped in with vital spares by cannibalising some of their other 'flyable duds', routine maintenance was done by 25 Maintenance Unit at Hobsonville but it took a week to bring even one Dauntless up into a flyable condition. Even with an all-out effort fewer than three or four aircraft could be kept in the air initially which seriously curtailed the strenuous efforts being made to get the squadron's training programme started, despite the allocation of US Marine Corps Master-Sergeant E. W. Carmichael as an instructor.

Another four SBDs were acquired to help over this difficult situation, but these were in little better shape and, in September, further urgings brought forth another five, giving the squadron a total paper strength of eighteen (NZ5010–NZ5018). This enabled a limited start to be made on familiarisation flights and conversion training of the assigned pilots, who came mainly from existing Army Co-Operation Squadrons and Anti-Aircraft Flights. A start was also made on introducing the Wireless Operator/Gunners to the Dauntless, most of whom were fresh from training courses in Canada. The various programmes gained momentum and were finally completed by 6 January 1944 when the squadron flew its full complement of 18 aircraft over Auckland, prior to embarkation.

Meanwhile, late in 1943, the squadron's Servicing Unit

sailed aboard the US transport *Octans* and established a forward base at Pallikulo, Espiritu Santo, the northernmost island of the New Hebrides group. The squadron arrived there on 31 January 1944 and flying training was immediately re-started. Between 7 and 13 January day and night flying prac-tice, dive-bombing, and gunner and beam practice was con-ducted from Espiritu Santo. The original aircraft had by this time been replaced by another 27 aircraft more recently ac-quired, this time SBD–4s (NZ5019–NZ5045).

Further training and 'tropicalisation' was carried out through into February by the squadron itself. By 6 February they had clocked up 40 hours 30 minutes of non-operational flying but this training intensified and resulted in the unit's first loss, NZ5037 (Flying Officer A. Moore and Flight Sergeant J. K. Munro). They had taken off at 13.45 for one hour's beam flying practice but became overdue. No trace was ever found of them.

Before moving into the combat zone, however, 25 Squadron was re-equipped again – on 11 February with 23 new SBD–5s (NZ5046 to NZ5068). The SBD–4s, as de Lange had made clear, were in no better condition than the SBD–3s had been and were not suitable for full combat duties. Ultimately the squadron began operations with 14 new and 4 reconditioned aircraft. The aim was to have the squadron ready for battle by the end of February in order to be established at Piva in time to forestall the coming Japanese operations, but this proved im-possible. A few weeks' further flying time was required to familiarise themselves with their new mounts, but that was all.

During the week 14 to 19 January the weekly flying time of 169 hours 10 minutes was made up by dive-bombing practices and beam approaches, including combined operations with 30 Squadron's Grumman Avengers and US Marine Air Groups 11, 12 and 21. One mass dive-bombing attack by all 102 aircraft took place on Cook Reef, to the south of the group, and other target areas included Sail Rock. Much valuable experience in methods of attack, rendezvous and break-up was gained at this time. Another 203 hours 50 minutes flying time was attained the following week and further exercises conducted with MAGs 11 and 12, while 49 hours 15 minutes time of practice flying was attained from 28 February to 5 March. From 6 March until the squadron departed for Bougainville, via Henderson Field, only a final 12 hours 15 minutes was achieved. The squadron took off from Pallikulo in two groups of nine aircraft. Staging through the famous airstrip on Guadalcanal cost the squadron its second loss when Flying Officer Graham so damaged his aircraft (NZ5055) on landing that it had to be written off.

The news from Bougainville was not good. Piva airstrip was being steadily bombarded as the Japanese concentrated their attack ever closer around the limited beachhead area. Extra enemy aircraft had been flown into the Rabaul airstrips from the Japanese main fleet and the Allies' position was becoming perilous in the extreme. The actual perimeter at Torokina at the beginning of March extended for about four miles along the coast of Empress Augusta Bay, and then ran inland from the beach to form a rough semicircle with a maximum depth of about three miles from the sea. The US 'Seebee' construction teams had quickly established three airstrips there, the original Torokina fighter strip, parallel with the beach, and a fighter and a bomber strip at Piva, 25 Squadron's destination, was built some two miles inland.

In late February US intelligence had intercepted a code message to the Japanese commander in the south-west Pacific ordering an attack on the perimeter on 7 March. The Japanese plan was to drive the Allies back to the beaches where a naval attack would, they believed, complete their destruction. Right on cue, at 06.00 on the morning of 8 March, the Japanese began an artillery bombardment and they continued with intensive shelling for the rest of the month. Lieutenant-General Kenda launched the whole of 6 Japanese Division into the assault in three columns and for a time they came perilously close to achieving their objectives. Into this cauldron moved the Servicing Unit of 25 Squadron, their arrival coinciding with the Japanese shelling of the perimeter. Almost immediately the men had to be organised into defensive infantry platoons and allocated positions in the third line of defence in case the enemy should break through. In between these alarms they tried to prepare the strip for the SBDs to arrive with the enemy only a few hundred yards from them. Much of the success of 25 Squadron's subsequent operations owes much to these men.

As their own report stated: 'The Squadron arrived at Bougainville when the activities around the perimeter were at their peak. The continuous shelling, particularly at night, and the noise of the return fire from our own guns prevented adequate sleep and rest. The shelling of the camp area and revetments while warming up and taxiing out for take-off, was another mental hazard.'

When the aircrew themselves arrived with their new aircraft all was ready. The squadron lost no time in getting their first sortie under way. Landing at Piva at noon on 23 March, they carried out their first operation at 05.30 the next morning. That day the squadron made 19 sorties: mainly bombing attack on enemy gun positions. The first two days' operations were intensive, and unique in the history of the RNZAF in that ground crews were given a grandstand view of the aircraft they were servicing actually dropping their bombs on enemy positions only 700 yards distant from their camp area. Being able to see the dive-bombers hitting back after being impotent on the receiving end for so long boosted their morale. This continued to be true even through more enemy shelling. For example, a total of 52 shells arrived in the camp area on the day of the squadron's arrival. Usually the shelling started at dawn. The SBDs would start up in the midst of it and, once airborne, would stooge around Japanese positions to pick up the flashes of the guns and so pinpoint them. They did not have to venture very far. In the first two days 18 aircraft and aircrews were operational out of 18. Thereafter the availability of units was kept high despite all the difficulties. On average the requirement was for some 12 aircraft, out of a normal total of 15, always to be kept serviceable. This objective was achieved and maintained for a three-month period, except for one day when they were one aircraft short.

Squadron-Leader de Lange made the first operational sortie, an artillery-spotting mission at first light, and five more such missions were flown over the next three days. The first true dive-bombing strikes were also very successful. Four SBDs co-operated with 12 from the Marine Corps VB305 squadron on 24 March with an attack on the enemy supply area at Tavera at the southern end of Empress Augusta Bay. Each New Zealand Dauntless placed a single 1000-lb bomb on the target and left a satisfactorily large pall of black smoke behind. A further 12 sorties were flown in support of the same Marine unit on another supply area to the east of Kamo Hill, which overlooked their airstrip at Piva. During both the first day's missions the squadron embarked Lieutenant Viggers, an officer from the 1 Fijian Battalion who was familiar with the island and who pointed out the target area to the flight leaders. Two dozen 1000-lb bombs on the hill left this officer very satisfied with 25 Squadron's first day's efforts.

On 25 March the 18 aircraft flew two dive-bombing sorties of nine planes each against local enemy gun positions and troop concentrations, the SBDs pushing on down in a 75-degree attack angle to within 2500ft before releasing their single 1000-lb bomb loads. One Japanese artillery battery was completely destroyed this day, 25 Squadron being credited with two direct hits. It was subsequently learnt that the Japanese colonel in charge of operations on Bougainville was killed in one of their strikes.

From the third day, 26 March, onward the New Zealand SBDs began to range further afield for, as well as defending their own base, they and the US Marine dive-bombers, under overall command of the American Admiral Halsey, were to take over the role of reducing the Rabaul and nearby island airstrips. From now on, although work on Bougainville never ceased, their main effort was directed against Rabaul and its myriad airfields. Flights of six or 12 aircraft were sent in with the US Marine Corps squadrons every day, except in bad weather. Vunakanua and Tobera strips were the most frequently attacked. Number 25 Squadron was so well assimilated into these actions that it became, both in operations and in achievement, an almost totally integrated US dive-bomber unit.

On 26 March the New Zealanders assisted the Americans in an attack on Kavieng, New Ireland, in support of the American

landings at Emirau, some 75 miles away, in order to neutralise
the enemy airstrip there. The attack was staged through Green
Island to co-operate with further Marine dive-bomber units
there but, on taking their departure, bad weather was encountered and 25 Squadron's aircraft, along with six Marine SBDs,
missed the rendezvous. After 2¼ hours they had to return to
Green Island. It was one of the very rare operations that the
New Zealanders were forced to abort.

On the following day one aircraft again had to return to base
out of a flight of six which attacked an enemy supply area at
Talili Bay. The enemy AA-fire was moderate but accurate but
only minor damage was received by the attacking aircraft. All
their bombs were reported as landing in the target area and
many fires and a large cloud of smoke resulted. That same day
Japanese supply and personnel areas inland from the mouth of
the Maririci River were attacked by six more SBDs. The actual
target area was covered with dense foliage and results were hard
to see; nonetheless 10 of their bombs hit the target area. The
dive-bombing attack was followed by a strafing run against the
same area and on an enemy supply barge spotted on the river
itself. Rabaul was attacked again the following day, the target
being Lakunai airfield. Thirty-six aircraft took part with 25
Squadron contributing its usual dozen planes, but, again, three
were forced to abort with engine trouble. The remaining nine
made confirmed hits on both the runway itself and AA-
positions in the face of intense fire which left one Dauntless
with a tailplane full of machine-gun holes. AA-positions were
again the targets of six of 25 Squadron's aircraft in an attack on
the enemy supply area at Vunapope on 29 March when three
direct hits were confirmed.

An established routine was beginning to emerge as these
strikes against Rabaul grew. The squadron's own Report details
the methods thus:

> The targets in the Rabaul area were in the main gun positions
> surrounding the aerodromes and supply areas. On four occasions
> the target was the supply area itself, and on three occasions the
> runway.
> The task of the SBDs during the attack is to knock out or

quieten gun positions in order that the TBFs (Grumman Avenger torpedo bombers being used by both the US Marines and 30 Squadron RNZAF as shallow dive-bombers) may have a clear run through to destroy the strip which is the primary target. This is accomplished by dive-bombing the gun positions which each aircraft is allotted and strafing further gun positions on the line of retirement.

Vanakanau airfield was the target for 36 SBDs and 24 TBFs on 30 March, with 12 of 25 Squadron's aircraft not only participating but providing the lead force. There was heavy cloud over Rabaul which partly obscured the target area and two aircraft had bomb hang-ups. Another was hit by small-arms fire on the way down. Ten direct hits were made despite the difficulties, however. Next day it was the turn of gun positions on Lakunai airfield. Twelve of the SBDs again joined with a total of 53 bombers, each contributing a 1000-lb bomb. The New Zealand aircraft were credited with three direct hits on the airfield and two damaging hits on gun positions.

The initial Japanese push against the beachhead had now been halted, but the enemy were still very active and 25 Squadron had to again turn their attentions inland on 1 April. Six SBDs made local bombing strikes on Japanese supply and bivouac areas near the Maririei River during the morning, and this was again the target for the remaining six the same afternoon. Again the weather intervened effectively with showers and clouds making location of targets difficult in the extreme, no resultant fires or smoke were observed after either strike. It was the same story on 2 April when another large strike was made with 66 SBDs and 24 TBFs against Rabaul. Again the joint attack was forced by heavy cloud to divert to the secondary target of enemy barracks and store buildings at Raluana Point. An estimated 41 bombs hit the target area, resulting in the destruction of many buildings, one very large, and many small fires. Supply barges at Keravia Bay were hit twice and other buildings along the beach were also obliterated.

This attack was notable (or notorious) in being the only time the New Zealand dive-bombers were partly bombed-up with 120-lb fragmentation bombs. One was fitted under each wing on Type-50 wing racks. They were not a great success which is probably why they were not used subsequently. One aircraft returned to base with both clusters hung-up and one with a single cluster hung-up, all of which were jolted free by the landing. As a result the safety devices of the M110 nose fuses shattered on contact with the metal strip and the explosion wrecked both aircraft (NZ5054 and NZ5059) and injured the pilot of the latter, Sergeant Symonds, and both navigators, Flight Sergeants Price and Boden.

On 3 April 25 Squadron again provided the lead squadron in an attack against gun positions at Vunakanua but again heavy cloud cover forced some pilots to turn their attentions to AA-guns at Tobera instead where a direct hit on one position was confirmed. Those that did attack the main target again found the conditions prevented them making accurate assessments of what damage they inflicted. On the following two days the weather closed right in, preventing any attacks being made at all. It did not, regrettably, prevent the squadron taking further losses. These came about in the following fashion. Two new Dauntless, still in their original US markings and codes (14 and 176), were waiting collection at Henderson Field, to replace losses and damaged SBDs. Accordingly, on 4 April, Flying Officers McLellan-Symonds, Graham and Howie (the former in an American aircraft, the two latter in NZ5048) flew down to Guadalcanal via Munda to collect them.

At 14.00 they left Guadalcanal with Graham piloting the new 14, McLellan-Symonds piloting 176 and Howie in NZ5048, to head back to Bougainville via a refuelling stop at Russell Island. Unfortunately the new aircraft's radio equipment was not functioning correctly as they flew northward and after a while they lost audible contact with each other. That didn't matter as long as visual contact remained, but the weather again began to close down and night was coming on. They missed their way heading up the 'Slot', overshot and recognised the coast of New Britain while there was still light. Immediately they turned back towards Green Island but 176 broke away, still uncontactable, and was never seen again. Both Graham and Howie eventually got their mounts down safely after a hairy night-landing an hour after dusk on Green Island and rejoined the squadron later.

Apart from the two tragedies, during the period of 15 March to 5 April (covering three weeks of the squadron's activities) the SBDs had achieved a great deal with little loss. The following was the squadron's official summary of guns they had destroyed:

5in. Dual Navy type	4
105mm	4
77mm	16
Auto	25
Light	42

One report read:

> In four instances heavy gun batteries have been brought closer together so as to utilise one set of fire-control equipment for two batteries of guns. This indicated that there has been great destruction of fire-control equipment such as height finders, long-range telescopic sights and speed and angle of course indicators. In addition the entire fire-control system of two batteries of 5-in. guns has been destroyed. Although no official figures for the period 15 April to 15 May have as yet been issued the number of guns destroyed is greater, as is evidenced by the comparatively few remaining still to be destroyed.

When the weather lifted on 6 April operations got under way again to neutralise the Rabaul airstrips. Vanakanua was attacked by 66 SBDs including the usual dozen from 25 Squadron, and 24 TBFs. Although cloud cover over the target again made the force switch targets to the Talili Bay supply area the strike was subsequently considered a very successful one and a number of Japanese gun emplacements were destroyed. The same areas were struck the following day, but this time only six SBDs from the New Zealand unit participated and these made their mark hitting six different gun positions and having three guns definitely confirmed as destroyed. On 8 April 25 Squadron again contributed six aircraft to a strike by 48 SBDs and 17 TBFs at Rataval ridge. Three direct hits were recorded on gun positions; five of them by the RNZAF Dauntless. Five more

SBDs mounted an attack the same day against Japanese artillery positions some 1000 yards west of the Mamgata river on Bougainville itself, scoring one direct hit and placing all their other bombs in the general target areas.

The Japanese 2 Carrier Division had landed huge numbers of its aircraft ashore there in January 1944, only to see them whittled away day after day in fruitless missions until their highly skilled carrier aircrews had almost wasted to nothing. Finally the emaciated squadrons were pulled out on 20 February, leaving the airfields almost empty, mere targets to divert the Allies' attention while they pulled back to Truk in the Carolines many miles to the north. The aircraft that remained to Admiral Jinichi Kusaka were 30 damaged Zero fighters and 26 bombers. Kusaka was told to hold out notwithstanding and his resolute response was 'Let's get to work.' So the Japanese garrison dug in and held on grimly as air attack succeeded air attack in a relentless and remorseless pounding. As an unsinkable aircraft-carrier, or as a bottomless sponge soaking up Allied aerial bombardment that might have been better employed elsewhere, Rabaul still remained effective. More, Kusaka and his team not only endured this but managed to repair eleven of the 'written off' aircraft to make audacious, if largely ineffective, harassing air attacks as far afield as Manus while still retaining aerial communication with their by-passed garrisons on Bougainville and New Ireland as well as Truk itself. It was a highly praiseworthy effort.

One eyewitness to the Allies' saturation raids was Father R. P. Poncelet, a Belgian priest interned at Vunapope. He recorded how 'the daily attacks continued. Clouds of American aircraft, bombers and fighters, arrived each morning. The sirens announced them with their strident whistling noise . . . From time to time we witnessed aerial battles when the Japanese fighters dared to sally out to the attack. We could see aircraft falling in flames, either diving off to the right or turning away slowly to disappear finally into the sea or the bush . . . One day I saw five aircraft swallowed up into the sea near Vunapope in several minutes.'

By the time 25 Squadron had joined in these raids the sight of any defending aircraft over Rabaul was a novelty. One such occasion was on 9 April when a solitary Zero was sighted off Cape St George by the 12 New Zealand SBDs which were leading a 60-plane strike against Vunakanua airfield gun positions. The Zero made no attempt to tangle with the mass of bombers or the eight escorting Marine fighters. Another enemy plane was sighted during the actual dive-bombing, a twin-engine machine squatting on the runway. Although most of the usual gun positions remained mute, four new batteries opened up and these received the bulk of the bombs planted that day. No less than eight of the SBDs were hit, including two of the New Zealanders: NZ5051, which had its starboard wing and tailplane badly peppered and the radio aerial shot away; and NZ5048 which took a cannon shell through the rear fuselage. All the aircraft made it back to base, however.

The next day 12 SBDs from 25 Squadron were part of a 40-plane force that struck at Raluana Point and Vunapope. They made their approach from 12,000ft and this time no less than four Zero fighters were sighted quite clearly by two of the squadron's wireless operators, Flight Sergeant Gray (NZ5056) and Flight Sergeant Bailey (NZ5060), some 1000 yards off to left of the Dauntless formation and slightly above it. An attack seemed inevitable but strangely the enemy pilots made no attempt even to harass the SBDs and broke away after briefly weighing up the odds.

With this threat behind them the dive-bombers continued with their normal attacks, pushing over from 9000ft and diving down to a bomb-release height of 2500ft. Three aircraft were hit by flak during the descent before breaking clear at 1500ft and carrying out the usual strafing attacks as they exited, via St George's Channel. As they did so they sighted another solitary Hamp fighter which proved equally unheroic. Three damaging hits were reported on the target buildings while the damaged aircraft (NZ5047, 5049 and 5061) all reached Piva North safely.

On the following day 50 bombers hit gun positions to the west of Simpson Harbour but were unable to see the results of their attacks. They did, however, spot a solitary Mavis flying-boat tethered to her buoy during the attack. What was probably the same aircraft was observed leaving the area the following day when the squadron led in another strike of 36 SBDs and 24 TBFs against gun positions along Talili Bay. They scored one direct hit and five near misses, without loss.

And so the work continued day-in, day-out, with little variation. Number 25 Squadron was operating under the direct control of the US Strike Command, COMAIRSOLS (Command of Air Operations, Solomons). Its Marine sister squadrons were from VC40, VB305 and VMSB235, and later VB306 and VMSB241, all from Marine Air Group (MAG) 24 under Colonel Lyle H. Meyer. Although the normal tour of operation was six weeks, 25 Squadron kept going for 8½ weeks. Moreover during this time the squadron carried out double the operational sorties per head of their US Marine flyer equivalents. The official report put this down to the lack of sufficient aircraft in the area, which both enforced the use of all available planes and required the squadron to provide 12 planes on a daily basis. Secondly there was the fact that Japanese fighter opposition was practically negligible. Previously the strikes had been governed mainly by weather. If the weather between base and target was at all doubtful the strikes were cancelled or the aircraft returned to base if already airborne. This was because their own fighter cover was unable to keep track of the SBDs and TBFs when flying through clouds and would have been unable therefore to provide sufficient protection in the event of Japanese fighter interceptions. With the falling-off of such enemy fighter opposition the weather became a secondary consideration and only a solid front between base and target or over the target area then prevented a strike from reaching its primary target. The average flight time for a strike on Rabaul varied between 3½–4 hours.

There was also the knowledge that there was no relief unit available anyway. The formation of the second dive-bomber squadron, 26 Squadron, had been authorised and Flight Lieutenant P. R. McNab, with two companions, was posted to a Dauntless unit working up Stateside to learn the ropes. However, on 13 November 1943 its formation was postponed, for ever as it turned out. The reason given was that there were too many different types of planes already in the small RNZAF. One of 26 Squadron's intended pilots, Flight Lieutenant J. R. Penniket, joined 25 Squadron in December 1943 to gain experience and he remained with them throughout their war tour.

Their routine continued for the next few weeks. Their losses remained minimal but on 17 April another Dauntless vanished. Twelve SBDs formed part of a 47–SBD and 30–TBF attack on gun positions adjacent to Lakunai airfield on Matupi Island and Hospital Ridge, on the Lakunai runway, and on the causeway between Lakunai and Matupi Island on the Gazelle Peninsula encompassing Simpson Harbour. The strike was met with heavy AA-fire but was considered successful with a large number of damaging hits confirmed on the guns. One Dauntless, NZ5058, received so much damage from flak on this mission that, although she reached Pavi safely, the aircraft had to be written off.

Worse still was the fate of Pilot Officer G. H. Cray and Flight Sergeant F. D. Bell in 'Prune's Progress' (NZ5050) which was last seen over the target. The Squadron Memorandum Book completes the story as far as it can ever be told:

> 10.30 – SBD Operations advised me that all aircraft had returned from strike with the exception of one of ours, 5050.
>
> 10.45 – SBD Operations asked AAC5 to signal Green Island and inquire whether 5050 had landed there
>
> 12.50 – Inquired from Fighter Control whether any information had been received regarding 5050. They told me that this aircraft had not landed at Green Island and that the Dumbo (a Catalina flying boat used for air-sea rescue work in the islands) had searched for two hours in the vicinity of a position given to them by Major Todd without result. This position was given over the radio by an aircraft intending to make a water landing.

On 18 April a 37-plane strike was mounted against Simpson Harbour led by six New Zealand SBDs but, again, conditions over the target led to a switch against the supply area at Rabanga Bay. Although five fighters were observed on the Raporo runway they made no direct challenge to the dive-bombers and the attacks were carried out in the face of light flak only, and only 31 of the bombs were reported as not hitting the target. Next day the weather was even worse over New Britain and a 48-plane attack led by nine of 25 Squadron's aircraft had to be aborted when still some 100 miles from the target on Matupi Island. Local attacks on 20 April and a repeat of the Matupi attempt on 21 April were both 'weathered out' and all planes remained grounded. When a big strike did manage to get airborne on 22 April, with 12 SBDs of 25 Squadron leading 42 USMC Dauntless and 24 Avengers against Vunakanua, cloud cover prevented them attacking either this or the secondary target of Lakunai, and they had to turn their attentions against Rapopo airfield, with 11 out of 12 bombs making direct hits.

Since they were working so closely with the US Marine Corps units and using the same aircraft, it was inevitable that 25 Squadron should adopt their methods of attack. The 'V' formation was abandoned for the US Diamond Box of fours during the approach period, and normal height was about 14,000ft. The initial descent would be made some distance from the target down to around 9000ft at speeds of about 270 knots. Over the target itself the final attack dive would begin from this altitude at a 75-degree angle with dive brakes extended, while bombs were released from heights of 2000 to 2500ft with pull-out at around 1000ft.

Almost all the attacks carried out by 25 Squadron were made with single 1000-lb bombs designed to crater the runways and smash guns and equipment. Fusing depended on the type of target pre-selected, usually 1/10th second. The underwing 100-lb bombs carried instantaneous fuses. Fragmentation targets were few and, as we have seen, the bomb carriers themselves were unsatisfactory. Occasional strafing runs were made as part and parcel of the attack escape routine in order to keep enemy AA-gunners' heads down at this critical point.

The week that ended on 23 April had seen 63 bombing sorties flown but only 30 of these, less than half, had reached the target because of the weather and on 23 and 24 April there was no flying possible at all. Next day 12 SBDs led a strike by 48 dive-bombers and 24 TBFs against Lakunai airfield and the adjacent gun positions on Matupi Island and Hospital Ridge, scoring many damaging hits. One aircraft, NZ5061 (Flying Officer F. G. McKenzie), was hit but not seriously. No less than 62 direct hits were made on their old target of Vunakanua next day and, out of the usual dozen New Zealand dive-bombers, one, NZ5049 (Flight Lieutenant T. R. F. Johnson), was hit in the propeller and had to force-land on Green Island. Two days' restricted weather conditions followed with a strike on Lakunai being forced to return on 28 April. The next day the primary targets for 48 SBDs and 24 TBFs was again Lakunai with, as secondary target, Matupi Island. Once again the weather prevented attack on either and the aircraft assaulted instead a military barracks and a native village on the east coast of Buka Island. All but 12 of their bombs landed in the target areas and a number of direct hits on buildings were reported.

Local flying was conducted on 30 April with 12 SBDs airborne to carry out artillery spotting for counter-battery work during the day, and the same schedule occupied them on 1 May 1944. The weeks that followed were generally of the same pattern with over 231 hours' flying time being clocked up by the squadron during which 66 sorties were mounted. Tobera air-strip was hit on 2 May. One aircraft had a bomb hang-up but the other 11 hit the runway. Vunakanua was re-visited on 3 May and one of the New Zealand SBDs varied the routine with a direct hit on the bridge at the mouth of the Warango river. In return three of the 12 aircraft were damaged by flak – NZ5060, NZ5063 and NZ5066. Sohana Island in the Buka passage was scheduled as the target for the next day but bad weather aborted the mission. On 5 May six Dauntless bombed through a gap in the thick cloud against local targets on Bougainville itself. A heavy AA-site in a clearing some three miles south of Sorum was one objective and the Muguai Mission the other, but the results could not be observed.

On 6 May a spectacular result was achieved by a direct hit scored in an attack on the Rataval supply area of Rabaul by NZ5056 (Flight Sergeant C. N. O'Neil). The 1000-lb bomb 'started an immense fire, thought to be a petrol dump'. There was a great upsurt of flame, then thick black smoke rolled up to a height of 4000ft and remained visible at a distance of 25 miles from the target.

On 7 May, while 12 aircraft provided missions for local artillery spotting, a six-plane strike was launched against Rantan Island, to the south of Bougainville. Four of the bombs fell in the target area but results were not observed despite the fact that two US Marine Corps Dauntless, with photographers on board, accompanied the strike and circled the area. A new target provided itself for their attention the following day, however, in the form of reputed heavy coastal guns (5in. navy guns) in a battery mounted at the ironically named Cape Friendship at the southern end of the island. 'Nothing of a military nature was seen,' however, during the attack although three bombs fell in the required target area. One SBD out of the five had to abort with engine failure.

After another idle day work resumed on 10 May with a dozen New Zealand aircraft as part of a strike by 18 SBDs and 12 TBFs against gun positions on Matupi Island and on Hospital Ridge. They were met with heavy and accurate AA-fire, as if the enemy had been husbanding his strength and waiting for them. A four-engined flying-boat observed in the harbour may just have brought in fresh stocks of AA-shells from Truk, but be that as it may it was the hottest welcome they had received for a long period and two aircraft, one SBD and one TBF, were lost. The Dauntless – NZ5051 (Flight Lieutenant J. W. Edwards) – was seen to drop its bombs on the gun positions allotted to it at Lakunai and to pull out of the attack dive very low over the runway. A few seconds later a large splash was seen in the middle of Greet Harbour. When the aircraft failed to rendezvous with the rest of the force afterwards it was assumed it had been hit during the retirement and crashed without survivors.

The momentum of attack continued remorselessly despite this. On 11 May 12 New Zealand SBDs were again part of a large force (48 Dauntless and 24 Avengers) directed against Vunakanua. Once more bad weather conditions were encountered over the target and the attack force divided itself over a variety of secondary targets. Eight from 25 Squadron hit supply dumps at Marawak, south of Piva, Bougainville, scoring hits with seven bombs; 5in. air-to-ground rockets were also used in this attack for the first time by the Marine aircraft. Some of the others hit Tobera airfield while three more attacked a bridge over the Warangoi river in New Britain, the remaining aircraft of this quartet being forced to abandon the attack with engine trouble. He jettisoned his bombs over the sea and made an emergency landing on Green Island.

A more ambitious sortie took place on 12 May, a double strike in fact. Out of a total force of 48 Dauntless and 24 Avengers, 25 Squadron put up the normal dozen SBDs and struck at targets in the Rabaul area. After hitting targets from Talili Bay to Raluana Point they landed at Green Island to replenish fuel and bombs, and then attacked native villages south of Sorum, on the north-east coast of Bougainville, on their return flight. Slight damage to one Dauntless was the only result from light return fire. No strikes were conducted the following day, although two SBDs did some artillery spotting work, but it was back to Vunakanua on 14 May as part of a 48-strong strike from which photographic reconnaissance revealed that direct hits had been made on the runway. Again a rare sighting of half-a-dozen suspected enemy fighters was made some five miles distant during the retirement but these contented themselves with aerobatics at a safe distance, as though they were small boys jeering a bully but keeping well out of arms' reach.

The squadron's period of combat action was now fast approaching its end. Long overdue for a rest after constant operating in the most trying circumstances, it mustered itself for a few more days' operations. It was already known they were due to pull out and most of the men were ready to do so. On 15 May six aircraft attacked the supply area at Chabai, in the north of Bougainville, scoring five hits on the target area but they could not see the results and the next day four SBDs led a glide-bombing attack close to Tovera when Talili was closed in by clouds. That afternoon the target was Bonin airfield, an enemy strip in the north of Bougainville where they scored three direct hits on AA-gun positions on the field perimeter.

The final strike conducted by 25 Squadron was made on 17

May, six aircraft taking part in a 35-plane force, three of which hit gun positions at Lakunai airfield while the others bombed supply dumps at Buka and oil barges in Simpson Harbour. The mission has been preserved for posterity on ciné-film as a photographer flew as passenger in NZ5049 (*WinniPu III*) with Flying Officer L. H. F. Brown. All the aircraft returned safely.

During the next two days all available aircraft were brought up to maximum serviceability for the flight home and on 20 May 1944, 17 SBDs lifted off from Piva for the final time. First stop was Renard Field in the Russell Islands. From here the crews were flown in Dakotas to Guadalcanal and then on to Tontouta and Whenuapai.

Unfortunately the squadron was never again actively employed. It was officially disbanded in May. A new 25 Squadron was formed in October 1944 under Squadron-Leader G. M. Fitzwater, but this was as a fighter-bomber unit with Chance Vought Corsairs. This squadron served at Santo Espiritu, Guadalcanal, Los Negros and Emirau until it, in turn, was disbanded in July 1945.

Although its active life was short its achievements, both in organisation and in striking at the enemy on its very doorstep, were worthy of the highest praise. Against the loss of six aircraft, only two on operations, the Douglas Dauntless of New Zealand's only dive bomber squadron could set these results: 498,800lb of bombs had been dropped and 108,000 rounds of .50 calibre and 217,000 rounds of .30 calibre ammunition had been expended. They had a total of 18 confirmed direct hits on enemy aircraft, and 30 reported direct hits, plus seven confirmed damaging hits and six reported damaging hits. They also scored 252 hits in the target area, with 106 unobserved, and only 46 hang-ups. The hits in the area applied to targets like supply areas, machine-gun nests and various automatic gun positions which were difficult to pinpoint from photographs and where it was necessary to bomb by geographical location.

New Zealand should be proud of its dive-bombers and the air and ground crews that kept them flying during that critical period, even if their achievements were largely overshadowed by subsequent Australian operations in the battle, which began a few months later, to clear Bougainville of the Japanese.

One of the ironies of that episode is that, having withdrawn the only specialised Commonwealth dive-bombers from the island, because it was believed that their role was declining in the Pacific, the Allies were forced to utilise, yet again, obsolete and makeshift substitutes in the form of the 18 Boomerangs and four Wirraways of 5 Squadron RAAF, which flew into Piva in November 1944 to take up the work of 25 Squadron.

8
No Place to Hide

The contrast between the dive-bomber pilots who flew from the US Navy's carriers against jungle targets and those who operated from the jungle airstrips – whether of Guadalcanal, Rabaul, Arakan, Nadzab or Bougainville – is a stark one. On the surface the carrier dive-bomber crews were to be envied by their brethren ashore fighting the same enemy.

True, over the target, the same odds stacked up against both, and men shot down over the jungles faced the same odds in trying to survive; but, once the attack was over, the carrier dive-bombers flew back to their comfortable billets in the Task Force, whereas those fighting from the jungle strips had to endure a pest-ridden, sticky, humid climate with no amenities.

But there were other aspects of the land-based jungle dive-bombers' lives. They did not have to make long cross-water flights to an uncertain location. Distances between island airstrips were known down to the last inch and could be allowed for, while the comings and goings of the Task Forces were often dictated by the nearness of the enemy fleet, the unpredictable weather and other factors. Also the carrier-based dive-bombers were living in quarters which could, in an instant, become a death trap, their funeral pyre. Packed with aviation fuel, bombs, rockets, ammunition, its own oil fuel, guns and magazines, highly combustible aircraft and fitments, vulnerable below the surface to the torpedo launched by torpedo bomber or submarine, and above the surface by their massive open, wooden flight decks (not armoured steel like the British carriers but just teak through which bombs fell like a knife through butter), these vast ships were the prime target of every Japanese bomber or kamikaze pilot. It was like living on a bull's-eye 900ft long by 90ft wide.

Whatever the differences, however, the dive-bombers of the Allies, whether land-based or sea-based, faced the same dangers once they reached their targets, and increasingly those targets were the jungle-clad islands leading up from the South Seas to Manila in the Philippines. Both were driving towards that common goal, as, in turn, they spearheaded the assaults that were pushing the Japanese back.

As part of this two-pronged approach to the Philippines it had been planned that both Morotai, the northernmost of the Halmahera group, between New Guinea and the Celebes, should be taken by General MacArthur's forces and Peleliu, in the central Palau Islands south-west of the Carolines and on the direct sea approach to Mindanao in the southern Philippines, should be stormed and occupied on 15 September. Once taken both of these advance positions would provide air bases to support the planned invasion of the Philippines in October 1944, when Mindanao itself would be the first objective in a step-by-step re-occupation. Palau had already been attacked the previous March. Thus it was to carry out its part in this grandiose scheme that Task Force 38, with its air groups under the command of Vice-Admiral Marc Mitscher, set sail from Eniwetok on 28 August 1944 to soften up the enemy preparatory to the Palau-Morotai operation. The Fleet was where Mitscher always affirmed it truly belonged, at sea. Since the bulk of the Japanese carrier-based planes had been destroyed at the Battle of the Philippine Sea the previous June, they had little to fear from the Japanese fleet. They would certainly welcome surface intervention, should the Japanese care to rise to the bait, but in truth the enemy was husbanding his fleet in readiness for the final battle in defence of the Philippines. Short of fuel, without air cover while more groups were being scratched together, the Japanese were in a desperate plight. Mitscher's intention was to give them no respite, no breathing space in which to build up their air strength again.

The huge assembly of warships of which was the US 3 Fleet consisted operated in four separate but linked Task Groups. Task Group 38.1, under Rear-Admiral J. S. McCain, included the fleet carriers *Wasp II* and *Hornet II* and the light carriers

Cowpens and *Belleau Wood*, escorted by three cruisers and 11 destroyers. Task Group 38.2, under Rear-Admiral Gerald F. Bogan, comprised the heavy carriers *Bunker Hill* and *Intrepid*, the light carriers *Cabot* and *Independence*, the battleships *Iowa* and *New Jersey*, flying Admiral William F. 'Bull' Halsey's flag, three cruisers and 18 destroyers; Task Group 38.3, under Rear-Admiral Frederick C. Sherman, included the heavy carriers *Lexington II* and *Essex*, the light carriers *Langley II* and *Essex*, the battleships *Alabama, Indiana, Massachusetts* and *Washington* (under the pugnacious Vice-Admiral Willis A. Lee), four cruisers and 18 destroyers; while Task Group 38.4, under Rear-Admiral Ralph E. Davison, consisted of the heavy carriers *Franklin* and *Enterprise* and the light carrier *San Jacinto*, with two cruisers and 13 destroyers. The carriers held some 1100 fighters, dive-bombers and torpedo-bombers.

Most of the dive-bomber squadrons aboard the carriers were equipped with the Curtiss Helldiver. The SB–2C–1C, which had joined the fleet during the summer battles, was now being phased out in favour of the much-improved SB–2C–3; *Enterprise* carried VB20s, utilising the new mark from August 1944 onward; and by October only one group, VB15 aboard *Essex*, was still flying the old model in combat.

The 'Dash 3' Helldiver featured the much more powerful R2600–20 engine which drove a Curtiss four-bladed prop and carried two 20mm cannon in the wings instead of the previous four machine-guns. These packed more of a punch for ground strafing, the dive-bombers at this stage of the war having little use for their wing guns for any other purpose. Nicknamed the 'Big-Tailed Beast', the Curtiss SB–2C Helldiver had earned itself a tough reputation among the fleet's aircrew as an awkward baby who needed careful handling. The original design itself had been plagued by a host of development problems, problems that were not all eradicated by the time it first joined the fleet; indeed at one stage it was recommended that those serving afloat be dumped ashore and the Dauntless re-adopted. After all the SBD did the job: 'slow but deadly'. Finally, however, the worst problems on the Helldiver were overcome, and thousands of the SB–2Cs began churning off the produc-

tion lines. Larger bomb capacity, longer range, heavier arma-
ment, if not a great increase in speed, marked its advantages
over the SBD, to which were added the whole host of technological refinements including radar. Gradually, in combat, the
Helldiver built up its own rugged character and the last two
years of the Pacific War were fought by the navy dive-bomber
crews mainly with this weapon. With it Halsey's pilots finished
off the Japanese navy in a series of sledge-hammer blows which
avenged Pearl Harbor and more.

From 31 August to 2 September aircraft from the carriers
struck at Iwo Jima (Jima means 'island') and Chichi Jima, in the
northerly Bonin Islands. These were not jungle targets but,
after this diversion to keep the Japanese guessing, the emphasis
of attack was switched back south again. From 6 to 8 September
all 16 of the Task Group's carriers were due to hit Palau in
advance of 'A' (Assault) day, as scheduled for the US 15
Division. Davison's Task Group, which had earlier struck at
the Bonins, joined in this but en route from their stop-over at
Saipan they also carried out air strikes on Yap. On 7 September
eight Helldivers of VB20 joined in an attack against trouble-
some nests of AA-guns set in concrete bunkers which had
claimed several American fighters during the previous day's
strafing missions. Something heavier was called for and VB20
carried the required weight.

The weather was clear over the target with just a few isolated
clouds at 1500ft which hardly troubled the flyers. F6F–5
Hellcats with rockets first suppressed the flak, then the Helldivers met no resistance as they dropped their heavy 'cookies' on
the guns' sites. Two escorting cruisers joined in by bombarding
Yap town and its environs. It was on this strike that napalm was
tried out for the first time from the carriers, but it did not prove
effective as half of the tanks failed to ignite on impact.

Palau island was softened up on 9 and 10 September, when
eight SB–2Cs of VB20 joined the Avengers in a strike at
Bablthuap along with fighters from both *Enterprise* and *Franklin*. Although the Japanese had no aircraft left of their own, they
were well dug in among the coral and the jungle. They had
anti-aircraft batteries hidden in the wrecks of sunken ships

resting on the bottom of Koror-Malakal harbour to the south, and which gave the impression they were worthwhile targets. Altogether, then, Palau was the Japanese equivalent of a baited trap awaiting the unwary. It was later to catch the Marines, but the first to find out its deadly potential were the navy flyers.

An attack by Air Group 20 arrived over this area at dawn and sighted a destroyer and a merchant vessel anchored close in to the thickly wooded shore. The VB29 Helldivers were led by Lieutenant-Commander George Davis 'Hoot' Gibson, their executive officer, as he dived down through a clear, brilliant sky towards these apparently ideal targets. Each Helldiver carried one 1000-lb and two 250-lb bombs. But as the dive-bombers plunged into their attack sequences a wall of light and medium flak suddenly hosed up at them from within the bowels of the 'ships' and from concealed gun emplacements in the jungle. The leading SB–2C was ripped open on its underside, although Gibson managed to release his bomb before the dive-bomber plunged into the lagoon. One parachute was seen to open but no trace of either the pilot, or his crewman and gunner, Burbeck, was ever found despite repeated searches.

Nor were these two the only casualties suffered by VB20 that day. Another Helldiver had its bomb hang up during the attack. Determined to plant it among the Japanese AA-crews the Helldiver positioned for another dive and the remaining six SB–2Cs made cannon-firing strafing runs to keep the enemy gunners occupied. Their plan worked and the bomb hit the target but during these low-level runs another Helldiver, that of Lieutenant Hughes, was hit and his gunner, Wayne Waymack, was shot through the head and killed.

One description of subsequent missions which the Helldivers conducted against the fortifications, gun positions and radio installations on these islands, sums up perfectly both the work and the difficulties of the carrier-based jungle dive-bombers:

> The dug-in enemy was invisible, his weapons camouflaged, his equipment, if he had any, hidden. The only indication of his presence was the sudden, brown smoke from a hillside and the fall of shot around his target offshore or the flare and dark billowings of a fuel dump hit by a lucky bomb. In order not to give away his gun

positions to the ubiquitous and eager aircraft, the Japanese cut the ratio of tracer ammunition to ball to almost zero. Pilots reported no AA but returned with holes in their planes.

Meanwhile the other 12 carriers from the first three Task Groups attacked airfields on Mindanao. The main objective was to soften up the Japanese airfields but they encountered little resistance. This was a considerable surprise. On 12 September, therefore, they switched their attacks for three days to the airfields of the Visaya group in the central Philippines. On 14 September, Task Group 38.1 hit Mindanao once more. This three-day period was given the Operational name of STALEMATE II. From one of the carriers of Rear-Admiral Bogan's 38.2 Group, the *Intrepid*, the work of the Helldivers of VB18 was typical of all the air groups during this phase of the assault.

On 13 September 1944 the take-off of Air Group 18 from the carriers' decks took place at 06.10 local time from a position in latitude 11 degrees 22 minutes, north; longitude 126 degrees 45 minutes east. The mission was to destroy all enemy aircraft and installations on the northern end of Negros island, the western-most of the central group. Accompanying the 12 SB–2C–3 Helldivers were eight F6F–5 Hellcats and six TBM–1C Avengers, the latter acting in the shallow dive-bombing role. The dive-bombers were each armed with one 1000-lb GP bomb, with a .1 nose and .01 tail fuse, and two 250-lb GP bombs, with a zero delay nose and .01 delay tail fuse. This was the first air strike to be made against Negros island and, in the absence of any recent photographs or other up-to-date intelligence, the identity of some of the targets was uncertain at the time and hard to check later. After take-off the 12 SB2C–3s rendezvoused with the eight fighters and 10 torpedo bombers of their own Air Group, and then Air Group 8 of similar composition, followed from *Bunker Hill*, which was leading the strike.

It was a 242-mile trip to the target, much of it across enemy-held territory. Total flying time to the target and back was about three hours and five minutes and the SB–2C–3s used up 252 of their 315 gallons of aviation fuel. En route to the target zone the Group climbed to 14,000ft. There was bright morning sun, with visibility at 20 miles. Some alto cumulus clouds were at 8000ft down to 1000ft. The Japanese defenders soon located this group and sent up their own fighters to dispute this infringement of airspace they had hitherto regarded as inviolate but the Hellcats kept all the Japanese fighters well clear of the bombers. They quickly became embroiled in a vicious dog-fight with a variety of opponents: Zeros, Hamps, and Oscars, and even a Pete float-plane fighter tried to get in on the act. The American pilots reported that the Japanese fighters could make tighter turns than they could, that they had lower speeds, but faster rates of climb. Despite this the eight Hellcats claimed nine of these opponents destroyed for the loss of one of their own. Even this was not due to enemy fighter opposition as the F6F-5 of Lieutenant James B. Neighbours, USNR, was hit by flak in the empennage which blew off its whole tail. The Hellcat spun straight in and exploded.

Over an enemy target the dive-bombers led the attack, diving down through clouds. The Helldivers carried out their dive attacks on an airstrip, believed to be Silay, and obtained enough hits to make the runway temporarily inoperative. As expected, enemy flak was encountered during this and subsequent attacks. It was of the medium type, impact fused shells ranging from moderate to intense, and some light machine-gun fire was also received on the way out. Five of the 12 SB-2C-3s in fact did not release because of the lack of a worthwhile objective. This was just as well because, during the retirement, another airfield was sighted which they believed to be Cadiz. This airstrip was crammed with planes, 20–25 being counted on the field itself and in the revetments close by. Thus the Helldivers were able to turn their bombs on this inviting target. At least two Japanese planes were destroyed by direct hits, with another pair probably destroyed or seriously damaged by the blast. The bombing was followed up by numerous strafing attacks which, it was estimated, took out several further enemy aircraft, two for certain, three probable and six damaged. Some 4850 rounds of .30 calibre machine-gun bullets were fired, and 3360 20mm cannon shells.

Three of the Helldivers were hit by flak, one took a light

AA-shell through the tail, a second had a 7.7mm machine-gun bullet through the right wing root, while a third took a hole through the port wing from a similar weapon which caused a slight oil leak. None of this was serious, however. As regards personnel the only casualty was from shrapnel when one of the Helldiver's gunners, F. P. Crevoisier, received cuts on two fingers of his right hand during the dive.

One of the Helldivers became separated from the main group and, instead, joined the Avengers in their attacks against Alicante airfield, which left craters in that runway. The Helldiver returned from the mission but the Avengers were not so fortunate. One of them, piloted by Ensign D. Laner, ignored squadron procedure not to go below 1500ft and pressed down to 300 to make a strafing run. The flak arched up and the starboard trailing edge of the outboard wing of Laner's aircraft burst into flame, apparently destroying airfoil characteristics. The plane crashed near the runway and Laner and his crew, Lankford and Krantz, were killed outright.

A second strike was launched between 14.28 and 14.33 that afternoon. It rendezvoused and proceeded at an altitude of 12,000ft and a speed of 150 knots True Air Speed (TAS) against the same group of targets. The bomb loads and the number of aircraft was the same for the dive-bombers but heavier fighter cover was provided after the lesson of the morning, 14 Helldivers accompanying them, but only eight Avengers armed with two 500-lb bombs each. This stronger protection, coupled with the bloody nose they had received earlier, kept the Japanese fighters at bay and, although a group of four were seen at 16.40 during the approach to the target, they did not engage but headed off to the northward.

The airfield selected for the second of the day's strikes by *Intrepid*'s Group was thought to be Fabrica. Again about 25 enemy aircraft were reported on the ground there, many of which had been damaged in preceding attacks by other Air Groups. The weather encountered over the target was light overcast and the larger expanse of the target airfield lent itself, therefore, more to a glide-bombing approach than to dive-bombing. Accordingly VB18 made their attacks at angles varying from 35 to 65 degrees with bomb release generally at 2000ft. The runway was hit many times and several of the Helldivers also made strafing runs afterwards.

The Avengers of VB18 followed the Helldivers down in 30-degree glide-attacks from 10,000ft down to bomb release at between 2000ft and 3000ft at speeds up to 310 knots, and the pull-out height averaged 1200ft. The absence of any AA-fire encouraged them to make low-altitude strafing runs as well and many hits were scored on parked aircraft. All the bombers returned to base at 2000ft and at a speed of 160 knots without any losses.

The lack of suitable aircraft targets led to a switch in tactics for some of the strikes on following days. The Task Forces pressed in yet closer in defiance of anything the enemy might do about it. Mactan airfield and the harbour at Cebu, the inner-most islands of the Visayas Group, were assigned to *Intrepid*'s flyers. Ten Helldivers took part, joining the Group and completing the rendezvous and form-up at 09.15 before departing for Cebu, bearing 259 degrees true from the carrier at a distance of only 180 miles. The visibility over Cebu island, when they arrived at 10.30 was clear, with 3/10th cumulus at 11,000ft. Other navy aircraft were already diving on targets in the harbour area and so *Intrepid*'s Air Group circled for five minutes waiting for a clear gap. Only a few aircraft were seen on the airfield itself, a Zeke, a Hamp and a Lily, but these were not worth the expenditure of bombs, so they were left for the fighters to strafe.

VB18 turned its attentions now to a variety of alternative targets. In each case dive-bombing was conducted down to a bomb-release height of about 2500ft although the harbour area was well obscured by this time from smoke from the targets ashore hit by the previous attacks. The Avengers made glide-bombing attacks on ships in the harbour but scored no hits. Five of the Helldivers selected the Oil Refinery of the Asiatic Petrol Company as their target and made three direct hits with 1000-lb bombs and six with 100-lb bombs. These hits were verified by the Hellcats above and the refinery, by now burning heavily, was listed as probably destroyed. Another attack was directed at a large warehouse on Mactan Island in Cebu harbour and this too was left seriously damaged by a direct hit. The final Helldiver target was a 1000-ton coaster in the harbour itself which was hit by one 1000-lb and two 100-lb bombs and left on fire and listing. There was again no attempt to intervene by enemy fighters and the AA-fire was described as 'meagre'.

The Philippines were proving something of a disappointment to Task Force 38: there were few targets available because the Japanese were holding back their aircraft for the more crucial stage of the fighting later. Further strikes were sent in, however, and this time VB18 was part of a force that hit Bacolod and Alicante, the airstrip at Silay, aircraft at Cadiz and shipping in the Janchates Channel. There was cloud over the target, alto cumulus at 8000ft which partially obscured it, so both conventional dive- and glide-bombing was made by the Helldivers with bomb releases again at 2500ft. The presence of many small cargo vessels in the channel was taken as an indication, along with previous such sightings on 12 September, that the Japanese were supplying their airfields on Leyte in readiness for the expected American invasion.

Some 2400 combat air sorties had been flown by the fleet's aircraft in this three-day period against what was expected to be the toughest shore targets approached by carrier aircraft to date. Two hundred enemy aircraft had been destroyed. The enemy did not even stand and fight when part of the once-feared Caroline Island group was taken over by the Americans. The atoll of Ulithi, in the western Carolines, was occupied by II Amphibious Force without opposition on 20 September in order to provide a new fleet anchorage closer to the Philippines than Majuro in the Marshalls. From the magnificent new harbour base here US 3 Fleet was only 1000 miles from Manila and 1400 miles from Okinawa, and it had advanced some 4250 miles towards Pearl Harbor.

The nearby island of Yap, which contained a powerful Japanese garrison, was also to have been taken in the original plan but, in September, it was decided instead to ignore it and to use the troops earmarked for its assault in the Philippines. So Yap was yet another fortress island left to wither on the vine, helpless to intervene in the next American stride forward.

A different story took place at Peleliu where a very bloody encounter took place. Defended by some 8000 troops of the Japanese 14 Division under Lieutenant-General Inouye, the island was honeycombed with caves and defence points, so strongly built in the rock that they were relatively immune to the protracted air and naval bombardment and practically concealed from the troops on the ground until they opened fire. Thus Major-General W. H. Rupertus, with 1 Marine Division, took heavy casualties from Day One onward while engaged in wiping out the Japanese garrison which fought literally to the last man until 25 November. Long before then reinforcement, in the form of 85 Division, had to be landed to relieve the exhausted and decimated ranks of the US Marines.

Replenishment then took place at sea, and 3 Fleet once more closed with the enemy's main land bases, striking at airfields on Luzon on 21 and 22 September, concentrating on the heart of the enemy defence complex, the airfields around Manila itself, and switching back to the Visayas group on 24 September.

As one contemporary account put it, 'On 21 September, while Radio Manila was playing "Music for Your Morning Mood", Admiral Mitscher's flyers began to peel off over Manila harbour, Cavit and Nichols Fields. The harbour was jammed with cargo ships and tankers. One fighter pilot who was part Filipino reported that Manila didn't seem greatly changed. Cavit was rebuilt, part of Dewey Boulevard was blocked off as an airstrip, there was a big concentration camp at Las Pinas village, shell-scarred Corregidor looked green again. The Japanese radio announcer began playing a vocal recording called "Butcher Boy for Me", then suddenly he interrupted his programme with a frantic announcement in English: "Attention, listeners, attention, listeners. This is an air raid warning . . .". As he repeated himself in equally frantic Japanese it became clear that Halsey's dirty trick department had really upset Manila's morning mood. A man-made tornado sent many of the ships to the bottom. An ammunition dump blew up. Later in the day mist closed in and spared a few enemy planes, and some of them attempted unsuccessfully to hit Halsey's carriers next day. But Japanese air power failed here as dismally as elsewhere.'

Far from encountering the heavy and prolonged air attacks they had expected to be directed against their ships, the Americans claimed the destruction of over 1000 Japanese aircraft, and the sinking of 150 ships totalling 20,000 tons, for the loss of 54 of their own aircraft in combat and 18 more in deck accidents. There is little doubt that these claims, which could not be substantial, were believed implicitly by the Japanese defenders.

One American pilot was shot down over his target, but he was subsequently rescued the same day. He had a chance to talk to some of his Filipino protectors during his brief stay and they told him that even on the ground the Japanese were much weaker than thought by the Americans. Only a handful of the enemy existed in the Leyte area, they told him.

As a direct result of all this information Halsey recommended to the Joint Chiefs of Staff of Quebec that the intermediate landing on Mindanao which was planned should be omitted as unnecessary and that the landing force should go straight into Leyte on the same day. This plan was ultimately agreed but despite the face that the Navy planes had scored as spectacular a defeat of Japanese land-based air power in September as they had of the enemy sea-based air power in June, the aircraft losses in the Philippines were quickly made good by fresh fleets of planes from the homeland. In fact the Japanese Fourth Air Army came from as far afield as China, Singapore, Burma, the Netherlands Each Indies, Japan and even Manchuria, the Japanese stripping their defences elsewhere because they knew that the battle for the Philippines was the crucial battle.

Early on, the Japanese High Command had anticipated that the Philippines would be the next main area of American attack. They also decided that, should they fail to hold the Americans here, then Japan would be cut off from their main supplies of oil, tin, bauxite and rubber. Thus, no matter what strategic lands they held south and west of the Philippines they would all ultimately be lost if the Philippines fell. The same applied to their air power and their fleet, so both were to be risked in a final gamble to sway the outcome. Even their fresh successes on the Chinese mainland during 1944 would also be wasted if the Americans established themselves ashore here. The heady talk of the 'annihilation' of Japanese shore-based air strength was therefore as premature as a later Japanese announcement that Halsey's fleet had been wiped out off Formosa. The battle for the Philippines was, in truth, to be no walk-over.

Meanwhile the US 3 Fleet continued its preliminary work in attacking potential Japanese air bases and concentrations of air power in areas far distant from as well as close to Manila, in order to disrupt as far as they could the enemy build-up and pre-empt its resources of air reinforcement and support.

The great carriers, therefore, headed north from Ulithi on 6 October and reached Formosa four days later. At noon on 11 October two groups, those of McCain and Davison, struck at Aparri, the most northerly airfield on Luzon, with a 61-plane force. Some 15 enemy aircraft were destroyed there. Then they turned to Formosa: 1378 sorties were flown from all the carriers on 12 October, 974 on 13 October, and 246 on 14 October. This finally provoked a furious and sustained reaction from the Japanese 2 Naval Air Fleet based there and the US fleet was subjected to repeated attacks. Despite the best efforts of the Japanese airmen, however, the Americans lost no ships at all, and their casualties were only two heavy cruisers damaged and 89 aircraft destroyed.

The Japanese mounted 881 sorties and claimed to have sunk 11 carriers, two battleships and one cruiser and damaged many others. They took huge losses themselves, some 321 aircraft in all. Despite this, many deluded themselves into thinking they had scored a decisive victory. Admiral Ozawa had more sense and withdrew a task group of three cruisers and eight destroyers, sent to finish off the 'defeated and retreating remnants' of Halsey's fleet. This, to all intents and purposes, was untouched and still consisted of 13 carriers, seven battleships, 10 cruisers and over 50 destroyers. The Japanese counter-attacks had achieved next to nothing.

On 15 October the Davison group returned to the Philippines and again struck at airfields north of Manila on Luzon.

Lieutenant Emmett Riera led nine Helldivers of VB20 from *Enterprise*, which was operating some 230 miles north-east of Manila, just before 09.00. Crossing the coast of Luzon at 15,000ft in frequent rainstorms they penetrated to within 40 miles of the target when 50 Japanese fighters intercepted them. As Riera himself recorded, however: 'Escort was superb; not a single enemy fighter approached to within gun range of the bombers and torpedo-bombers, either during the approach or the retirement; every plane that attempted an attack was either shot down or driven off.'

Heavy clouds covered the Manila area and blanked out the airfields down to 2000ft. Dive-bombing was out of the question and the Helldivers had to do their best with low-level passes instead in the face of the most intense flak most of them had yet encountered in the Pacific. Despite this they caught the Japanese flat-footed and deposited their heavy bombs in among the rows of parked fighters.

Ozawa was to record, 'Again the carrier attacks frustrated our attempts to re-establish a defensive fighter force. Not only did we fail in every attempt to reinforce our fighter groups in the Philippines, but we could not even maintain our minimum strength.'

Japanese aircraft, 130 in all, struck back at the Task Group without much effect. Off Luzon the Japanese dive-bombers managed to break through and an attack by three of the new Judy dive-bombers and a Zero armed with bombs scored hits on the *Franklin*. Despite this she was operating her planes again the same day. A further 107 sorties were flown by the Japanese on 17 October while their 1 Navy Air Fleet in the Philippines failed even to find the carriers at all. Meanwhile on this day and the next the carrier aircraft again ranged freely over Luzon.

Manila was again hidden under thick cloud and the first strike force, which included 16 SB-2Cs from *Enterprise* and *Franklin*, had to circle the target for an hour until they found a hole through which to attack Mabalacat East airfield, part of the Clark Field complex. Twenty-eight enemy aircraft were claimed destroyed. Later the same day a second strike hit

Legaspi Field, at the southern end of Luzon, with similar results. On 18 October Helldivers from the same group attacked others of the Clark Field strips as well as the main airfield, and employed a new tactic – attack dives going in at 4500ft for bomb release and then following this up in the same steep dive with 20mm cannon fire. With the pilots able to concentrate on their wing cannon higher accuracy was attainable and good results were obtained against Japanese aircraft tucked away in revetments on the airfield perimeters. Another 18 Helldivers struck at Nielson Field and the harbour area that same forenoon with similar results.

Not content with this, a third force was dispatched at 13.30 that day by carriers of the Davison group, but this time the dive-bombers' targets were the more traditional ones of packed Japanese shipping in Manila Bay. A huge tropical storm was building up as they approached which caused them to divert, but eventually the combined force arrived over the target and began to circle counter clockwise, seeking their targets. Lieutenant Riera again led in the Helldivers but, as a consequence of the rain and wind, they again had to approach in glide-attacks against at least a score of large transports from a height of 12,000ft. They made their bomb releases at heights which varied from 1000ft down to as low as 500ft, and again utilised their heavy cannon to strafe as they pulled out across the bay through the intensive AA-fire. This found a victim in one SB–2C, piloted by Ensign Les Hornbeak, which crashed in flames in the Bay. At least five of the big ships were hit by 1000-lb bombs. The attack was over by 17.00 and the surviving aircraft began to rendezvous in the murk for the long flight back.

After four hours airborne, however, fuel was low, especially as another diversion was necessary to avoid the thunderheads which interposed themselves between them and the task group. Despite the fact that *Enterprise* steamed hard to close the gap it was dark when the straggling aircraft reached her. Some never made it. One SB–2C was forced to ditch at some distance from the fleet, three more had to pancake into the water close alongside. Destroyers from *Enterprise*'s screen eventually rescued all these crews.

The final strikes were made on 20 October against the small field at San Pablo, and they also hit Dagami town near the beachhead. With the army established ashore, the close-support work was to be left to others. Halsey's dive-bomber crews were pulled out to prepare to meet any intervention by the main Japanese Fleet. The result was the Battle of Leyte Gulf at the end of October 1944, the largest naval battle in history, in which the American ships and aircraft thoroughly defeated the Japanese.

In later operations the failure of conventional dive-bomber attacks to penetrate the huge wall of flak over the American fleet led to the standardising of the kamikaze form of air attack. Even so, many conventional dive-bomber sorties did take place, and, despite the odds against them, some of the Japan-ese dive-bomber crews based ashore, did manage to get through to their targets, although few survived to tell about it afterwards.

Many American carriers were hit, and almost always heavy casualties were caused whether they sank or not. So, it is worth reminding ourselves, lest all our sympathies lie with the island-based dive-bomber squadrons, what happened to two carriers, *Wasp II* (CV18) and *Franklin* (CV13) early on 19 March 1945, off Japan when their dive-bombers were operating against enemy targets in the Inland Sea. They were taken under vigorous counter-attack by the Japanese 5 Naval Air Fleet and a direct hit was made on *Wasp* which was set afire. There were 101 men killed and 269 injured by the blast and the resulting fires but, despite this casualty list, the carrier managed to bring the flames under control within 15 minutes.

Worse, however, happened to *Franklin*. Two-thirds of her air complement had already been launched at dawn but there were still five Helldivers, 14 Avengers and 12 Hellcats spotted on her wide decks at 07.08. They were fully laden with 1000-lb and 250lb bombs, and 'Tiny-Tim' 11.75in. rocket projectiles; and all were fully fuelled up, with their engines turning, awaiting take-off. The scene could have been that aboard the Japanese carriers at Midway just before the Dauntless squad-rons struck.

The results were certainly the same. A single Judy dive-bomber slipped out of the 2000ft cloud base, evaded the Combat Air Patrol, and made a dive-bombing run against the carrier, releasing two 250-lb bombs both of which were direct hits. The bombs, rocket warheads and aviation fuel all ignited in a gigantic explosion which rocked the great ship to her very keel. An eyewitness, Lieutenant Jim Hardin, a Marine radio correspondent, described the scene in this way:

> There was a tremendous explosion. Instantly a great ball of flame shot along the hangar and flight decks. Great clouds of smoke billowed as the carrier turned out of the wind. Then there were heavy explosions on the flight deck. In a few minutes the entire ship was engulfed in smoke, broken only by the glare of the explosions. Debris was landing in the water 500 yards from the carrier . . . At the edge of the deck I found two Marine pilots helping each other; one had a broken ankle. A large section of the flight deck exploded a few feet away . . . A terrific explosion lashed out when the planes still on deck disappeared as a bomb exploded . . . Their rockets fired and flashed behind in great orange streaks over our heads . . . The carrier shuddered as though in an earthquake . . . it seemed impossible that the carrier could remain afloat . . .

But remain afloat she did. Slowly and painfully she was towed out of the battle zone. Aided by the cruisers *Sante Fé* and *Pittsburgh* Captain Gehres brought his crippled ship back although for two days the Japanese attempted to finish her off. But she came through, though at what cost! Those two small bombs, delivered in one of the last Japanese dive-bombing attacks of the war, killed 724 men and injured a further 265, some horribly.

By their achievements and fortitude the men of the US Navy carrier squadrons carry the right to join the other jungle dive-bombers on an equal footing. Their main task remained, however, the destruction of the enemy fleet. To give the soldiers and Marines ashore the best possible close aerial support against a cunning and courageous enemy, who had become adept at using the jungle for natural cover, a more specialised unit was required. Thus the clock was put back by almost two decades and, once more, it was the flyers of the US Marine Corps who stepped forward to show what close support in jungle fighting really meant.

9
The Philippines Regained

In the steady closing of the ring by the Allies on the conquered territories held by the Japanese from the Solomons in the south round to the distant Chinese and Burmese borderlands, the dive-bomber played a leading role. The conditions of fighting in that vast zone, much of it covered by jungle, meant that precision counted for far more than overwhelming air strength. Attacking jungle-covered targets required that the bomb loads be delivered exactly on target to be effective, and only the dive-bombers of all the nations involved could regularly and unfailingly guarantee to do this. One of the leading exponents of this had been the US Marine Air Groups (MAG), operating first from Guadalcanal, then on Bougainville, and later in the Marshalls. It is no surprise, then, that the same flyers were in the lead when the basic techniques for close-support aviation, using dive-bombers, were absorbed, modified and then encoded; and it was in the re-conquest of the Philippines that the Marine Corps put all the lessons that had been learnt into impressive practice.

With the MAGs the Allies had, for the first time in the war, an equivalent integrated dive-bomber force that could instantly and accurately respond to the needs of the men on the ground in the same way that for years the German Ju 87 Stukas had been operating. It had been a long hard road for the Marine Corps flyers to fight, but the German blitzkrieg during 1939–41 had patently demonstrated the power of the dive-bomber if accompanied by effective radio links. Although this had alerted the United States Army and Navy to the effectiveness of the method and had re-kindled some interest in dive-bombing and dive-bombers as such, the Army's had turned lukewarm after tentative efforts in 1942.

The US Army Air Corps under General 'Hap' Arnold, had ordered large numbers of dive-bombers, but, after 20 years of neglecting the subject, it found itself in the same position as the RAF and had to poach its dive-bombers from other sources. It took batches of the A31 Vengeance from existing RAF orders, 300 aircraft in all, but then imposed so many modifications on it that it was virtually turned into a different aircraft, the A–35 Vengeance, of which huge numbers were ordered. However, the many modifications they insisted upon so delayed its entry into service that they were finally forced to abandon it.

The Army also ordered 100 land-based equivalents of the US Navy Curtiss SB–2C Helldiver, under the designation A–25A Shrike. By the spring of 1941 a procurement order for another 3000 had been placed and a new plant in St Louis to build them. The first A–25A flew on 29 September 1942. The first batch of 10 were completed in March 1943 by which time the USAAF had given up on specialised dive-bombers almost completely.

They ordered 192 of the Brewster SB–2A dive-bomber, again under development for the RAF. They named it the A–34 Buccaneer. But development work was so slow that the contract was cancelled before any machines had been produced. Finally the US Army Air Corps ordered land-based equivalent of the SBD Dauntless under the designation A–24 Banshee and equipped 8 and 91 Bombardment Groups with it. These were used in combat in the Dutch East Indies and with 27 Bomb Group operating from Australian bases against targets in the Timor Sea and New Guinea areas at Lae and Salamaua early in 1942. But having the aircraft did not mean that they knew how to employ it, and none of these operations was very effective. The last straw came when six out of seven A–24s were lost in an attack on Buna carried out on 29 July 1942. The Army claimed the A–24 was old, obsolete, unmanoeuvrable and slow. It was withdrawn from combat.

The only real dive-bombers that the USAAF finally received and actually used successfully in combat were the Mustang adaptations, the A–36A Apache or Invader. Some 500 of these had been used to great effect in Burma and China, and they were also used in Italy. But apart from these few air-craft the USAAF experience of dive-bombing had been far from a happy one. They concluded that it was not effective, was too dangerous (to the troops being supported as well as the air-crews) and too expensive. An official report commented: 'It is easy now to criticise the Army airmen for their lack of foresight, but their reactions must be placed in time and context. Striving for their independence they recoiled from too close ties to the ground forces – the idea was separation, not closer amalga-mation. Even the very term "Air Support" was an anathema to them. "Support" implies a secondary role – and through the war the preferred terms for tactical missions in direct support of ground troops were "air to ground co-operation" or "air to ground co-ordination".'

Army airmen considered control by infantry officers 'an attempt to shackle the air to the ground and therefore a failure to realise the full capabilities of air attack'. The Army Air Corps Field Manual, *Command and Employment of Air Power* (FM100–20, p. 12), as late as July 1943 could still enshrine their concept of close support as, 'In the zone of contact, missions against hostile units are most difficult to control, are most expensive, and are, in general, least effective. Targets are small, well dispersed, and difficult to locate. In addition, there is always a considerable chance of striking friendly forces.'

It was left to the Marines to show the way. Robert Sherrod had recorded that the main lessons learnt by Marine Corps flyers up to that period were:

1. Adequate and reliable radio communication from air to ground was essential. One-channel radios were entirely inadequate and later two-channel installations were not much better.

2. Panels and pyrotechnics (i.e. light signals and Verey lights, respectively, for example) were inferior to radio communications but often had to be resorted to because of poor radio equipment and radio discipline. Their use required thorough air-ground co-ordination.

3. An airborne co-ordinator was required for liaison be-

tween scout bombers in the air and infantry assault on the ground.

It is interesting to compare these requirements with the practice of the Luftwaffe Stuka units throughout the war. It is almost identical. Stuka pilots were sent in rotation to act as ground liaison officers to co-ordinate attacks, often leading Panzer columns in specially equipped tanks and calling in the Ju 87s whenever the enemy tried to take a stand.

Tentative experiments had been carried out by the US Marines to put into effect some of these ideas during the Solomons and Bismarck Barrier campaigns. These took place at first with their own Marine Infantry, then it was gently extended to their Army brethren. At Guadalcanal the Marine flyers had their first taste of jungle dive-bomber operations in support of ground troops. Many of their targets were warship and transports at sea, but they were also called upon to act as the only effective bombers to break up Japanese land attacks or silence Japanese artillery positions.

For the first two weeks at Henderson Field Major Richard Mangrum's VMSB 232 had to work in the most primitive conditions. There were no bomb hoists, for example, and the 500-lb weapons had to be manhandled from storage dump to aircraft revetment and there be hand-loaded on each machine. The hard rubber wheels for carrier landings turned the actual airstrip into a quagmire which torrential rain and enemy attacks from land, sea and air only worsened. The jungle climate, the insects, malaria and other diseases, all took their toll on the Americans as they had on the Japanese, British, Australians and New Zealanders who fought the jungle war.

As the Solomons campaign progressed the problems of how to pinpoint enemy gun emplacements – which had become more and more sophisticated – was another lesson to be learnt the hard way. What was soon obvious was that dive-bombing was the only effective way of dealing with this problem. Native scouts deep in the jungle reported back to dedicated Australian 'coastwatchers' as and when the Japanese constructed their gun positions and carefully hid them. Knowing where they were and actually hitting them were two different problems however. The Army medium bombers took their turn, to little or no effect. Then the Marine dive-bombers took a hand. The comparisons were enlightening. As Commander Eric Feldt, RAN, recorded in his book *The Coastwatchers*: 'Indiscriminate bombing of jungle positions is generally harmless, but this precise delivery of high explosives on selected targets was something else again.'

The same cry was to be heard time and time again in future campaigns down to Vietnam and beyond. The next step conducted by the US Marine Air Groups took place during the New Georgia campaign. What was described as a rudimentary system of close air support was devised. The term 'close support' was defined by the Marine Corps as being within 1000 yards of the front line. There were no specialists in air-to-ground liaison in the Pacific at this time and so volunteers were called for. These formed Air Liaison Parties under Major Wilfred Stiles. He had eight Officers, two from the ground forces and six from the Marine flyers, and eight enlisted radiomen. Stiles commandeered four command cars which he equipped with a SCR193 radio set, an Aldis signal lamp, some pyrotechnic gear and Isenburg cloth, used to cover (and uncover) the panels.

These teams were sent out to the front line in readiness on the Munda battlefront, but the soldiers were still far from convinced of the effectiveness or safety of such support. All fighting in the jungle was bound to be of a close hand-to-hand nature with limited visibility. In the dense terrain marking enemy positions was difficult even for artillery to home in on. As in Burma smoke marking with mortars was the solution. Map co-ordinates were also given. Like the artillery positions, only even more so, pillboxes and hidden foxholes were such that only direct hits would eliminate them.

However on 12 July 1943 the 169 Infantry Division found itself under intense flanking attack by an unseen enemy force and was pinned down. This was the first test of the new system. As might be expected it did not work as planned. The map co-ordinates broadcast to the airmen were not the same locations as the area picked out by the smoke mortars, in fact it was incorrect by some 600 yards.

Not until 1 August was another call made. The US 43 Division was in position to the east of the Lambeti Plantation in New Georgia, with Japanese artillery dug in on the north-east corner subjecting them to concentrated power and stopping their further advance. A striking force was called up by one of Stiles' teams which included 18 Dauntless dive-bombers and these delivered a crushing attack on the enemy positions.

Thus encouraged a third call was made on 25 August against a strong Japanese anti-aircraft position located on top of Bible Hill. No less than 54 SBDs, supported by 53 Marine and Navy Avengers, again acting as bombers. After the smoke of this devastating concentration had cleared the enemy positions were reported as being 'thoroughly silenced'.

As well as with conventional dive-bombers the US Marine Corps was beginning to experiment with the powerful Chance Vought F4U Corsair fighter-bomber in the dive-bombing configuration. The first unit to fly these big planes thus was the US Navy's VF17 against Rabaul in February 1944. In March the Marines of VMF11 equipped with the same aircraft fitted home-made bomb racks to their Corsairs and conducted trials. Dives of up to 85 degrees were found to be effective and the F4U reacted well. All-up weights of bombs in excess of those carried by the SBDs were soon being carried and the added punch of the six. .50 calibre wing guns was an extra bonus to be used for strafing during the pull-outs. On 18 March 1944 the first Marine Corsair dive-bombing attack of the war was delivered against AA-gun positions on the island of Mille.

In the by-passed Marshall Islands Marine flyers with MAW4 also employed the Corsair to good effect against Japanese positions on Maloelap and other atolls over a nine-month period. Rear-Admiral De Witte Ramsey was to write that:

> Over 75 per cent of the targets have been of 50ft or less in diameter whereas the normal dive-bomber target is 200ft in diameter. The targets in the main were Japanese gun positions which were eliminated one-by-one . . . The Marine squadrons involved tried

several techniques but the most effective for the Corsair seemed to be a 70- to 80-degrees dive at high speed.

One Marine pilot was asked if he would like to try this technique against German targets. His reply was, 'If they asked me to bomb a factory my first question would be – What department?'

It was known that the campaign to clear the Philippines would be a very tough one. The jungle was still there but there was also an urban element as well demanding house-to-house fighting with similar calls for precision as at Stalingrad. Because the Army obviously had no expertise in such methods it was decided early on to leave this work to the Marines. A much expanded Marine Dive-Bomber Wing was to be formed and trained up especially for the job.

On 10 October 1944, therefore, Colonel Lyle H. Meyer, commanding MAG24 on Bougainville Island, assembled his men and announced the part they were to play in the forthcoming battles. They were to be joined by MAG32 under the command of Colonel Clayton B. Jones, with veteran Marine dive-bomber pilot John Smith returning from the States as his executive officer. This gave the new dive-bomber Wing a total of seven SBD squadrons acting in concert. As senior officer Colonel Jones became overall commander of the Wing when both groups worked together in combat.

Assembling the aircraft and the men was the first stage. The second was the detailed assimilation of every close-support technique and theory known at that time and its formulation into a positive policy. This vital work was entrusted to a team headed by Lieutenant-Colonel Keith B. McCutcheon, MAG24 Operations Officer. He was to become the Marines' guru or 'don' of close-support systems.

One of the positive advantages of this arrangement was that the seven squadrons could devote their whole time and energy to this one subject. There was no need to break up the specialised training to cope with other eventualities, and, as in so many other war activities, it was found that one specially trained and close-knit unit was worth many generalised and all-purpose ones. Morale and understanding became indivisible, and there was the 'pride in unit and achievement' bonus that they were experts undertaking a vital job. Thus the dive-bomber wing dismissed long-range bombing missions and its associated problems from their minds, likewise air defence, all of which could all be left to others.

The unit also had another advantage in that the US Army 37 Infantry Division on Bougainville had experienced something of what they could do, and so had faith too in what they might be able to do better in the future. They therefore co-operated fully in the Marines' training programme.

Although the newer Curtiss SB–2C Helldivers and Chance Vought Corsairs were generally available, the Marine flyers were initially stuck with their faithful SBDs. These were reliable, and speed was not a vital element in close support, a fact which the Junkers Ju 87 in Europe had proven (and the APD Skyraider was later to prove in Vietnam). Accuracy, the ability to linger and deliver the goods where it was needed, these were the vital elements, something which most Allied Air Chiefs, armchair strategists and post-war 'experts' alike seem not to have fully understood.

Those on the spot at the time, and actually charged with doing the job, had no doubts however. They began work quickly. The tactics were studied, written out with diagrams and lectures, and printed for special courses for aircrew. No less than forty of these lectures were thus prepared *in three days*. Then, on 8 December 1944 study began for a total of 500 pilots and navigators/gunners who went through and absorbed all of 'Professor' McCutcheon's lectures. A basic close-support manual entitled *Close Support Aviation* was issued, which codified these methods and tactics.

The principle used by McCutcheon was that such close dive-bomber support was 'an additional weapon to be employed at the discretion of the ground commander' and was to be used by him as he saw fit 'against targets that cannot be reached by his other weapons or in conjunction with the ground weapons in a co-ordinated attack'. The guiding principles were that such close support should be, 'immediately available' and should be carried out 'deliberately and accurately' and 'in co-ordination with other assigned units'. This called for the teams to go forward with the lead troops in any assault so that they could familiarise themselves with the actual battle terrain because working just from maps was of insufficient use. Acting on bitter experience hardly re-learned, special emphasis was placed on radio communications and no less than four Communication Nets were set up to cover all eventualities. These were worked in conjunction with the improved Air Liaison Parties (ALP) which were now to be allotted the latest radio-equipped jeeps.

The radio nets are perhaps best summarised as follows:

SAR (Support Aircraft Request): this linked the ALP to the Support Aircraft Commander (SAC) and also the Airborne Air Co-Ordinator (AAC).

SAD (Support Aircraft Direction): this was a two-way channel to link the SAC, the AAC, and the supporting aircraft.

SADE (Support Aircraft Direction Emergency): as the name implied, this was an emergency channel linking the ALPs direct with the supporting aircraft.

SAD (Support Aircraft Observation): this was another two-way channel to link the SAD with the airborne observers in scout planes.

There were also four Very High Frequency (VHF) and two Medium High Frequenty (MHF) channels available to each SBD and to each ALP jeep.

The new tactics were given a pre-embarkation workout with the help of 37 Division while the Marine flyers were still on Bougainville. The soldiers simulated infantry attacks on an enemy pillbox and the ALPs in close attendance were able to tune in their nets as the SBDs conducted mock dive-bombing attacks in conjunction, but without dropping any bombs. Quite what the Japanese defenders thought about it all is hard to imagine but it was their colleagues defending the more important Philippines who were to 'benefit' from the lessons learnt. The exercise also increased the mutual respect of the dive-bomber crews and the infantry, a vital ingredient if the work was to prove ultimately worthwhile.

Everything, then, was as ready as it could be for the ultimate test of combat. Meanwhile the first army units had waded ashore on the disputed island on 17 October, with the main landings following up three days later on Leyte's east coast. On 21 October the first Marine force joined in the fray when Brigadier-General T. E. Bourke's V Amphibious Corps Artillery disembarked with 1500 Marines at the Leyte beachhead, not made fully secure until after the tremendous air/sea battles offshore had decimated what remained of the Japanese navy. The first Marine Aviation ashore was the Night Fighter Squadron VMF(N)541 which occupied Tacloban Field on 3 December. Meanwhile the SBD crews were still assimilating their lessons and awaiting their chance.

This finally came in the new year. During the last week of January 1945, five of the Marine Dauntless squadrons flew some 255 sorties and dropped 104 tons of bombs for the loss of one SBD shot down by AA-fire on 28 January.

Then the main Marine air units, including the newly readied dive-bombing squadrons from 1 MAW began shifting their emphasis to one of preparation for the army's forthcoming invasion of Luzon. On 9 January, the US 6 Army landed on that island and, two weeks later, units of MAG24 arrived. Shortly afterwards they began flying combat missions in support. At the Lingayen landing the first combat missions started in earnest.

The first large-scale tests took place, however, on 31 January when the Marine aircraft were ordered to give their close support to 1 Cavalry Division's drive to take Manila itself. In the 66-hour dash and in the subsequent fighting for control of the island the Marine aviators demonstrated to the full their newly found proficiency in the use of dive-bombing support. This practical application of the air-to-ground team proved to be very effective indeed and finally won over the army. One account read: 'The air support given by the Marines forced the enemy to remain under cover, helped to thwart his potential to establish effective resistance, and facilitated the rapid advance of 1 Cavalry Division.' Brigadier William C. Chase, commanding 1 Brigade during the advance on Manila said: 'I have never seen such able, close, and accurate close support as the Marine flyers are giving us.' Another distinguished army officer was of the same opinion. In an interview given after the Americans had entered Manila, Major-General Verne D. Mudge stated:

> I can say without reservation that the Marine dive-bomber outfits are among the most flexible I have seen in this war. They will try anything and from experience with them I have found that anything they try usually pans out. The Marine dive-bombers of the First Air Wing have kept the enemy on the run. They have kept him underground and enabled us to move up with fewer casualties and at greater speed. I cannot say enough in praise of these men of the dive-bombers . . . for the job they have done in giving my men close support in this operation.

The US Army pushed forward after Manila fell with 1 Infantry Division, under Colonel James R. Rees, taking San Jose to the north of the city on 4 February. On this same day Army Air Force aircraft had tried their hand at close-support strafing with the unhappy result of 1 Division taking several casualties from 'friendly' fire. This not only had an adverse effect on the troops but their commander was reluctant to repeat the experience, no matter how difficult things became.

However, on 28 February, a squad of soldiers under a wounded Lieutenant became cut off from the rest of their unit across a Japanese-dominated valley. The terrain was wild and difficult and the enemy were entrenched in positions as close as 200 yards to the encircled Americans. Any attempt to reach them, it was estimated, would take at least an hour under heavy fire. The parallels with Rowell's action of twenty years earlier are remarkable and the Marine Corps flyers were not slow to repeat the basic lesson of those days.

The Marines radioed an offer of help and, after a detailed briefing on the situation via the communications net, the soldiers' commander, Colonel Rees, gave them his permission to go ahead, but only by the dropping of a solitary wing bomb from each aircraft. It had to be right or not at all. The Marine flyers grabbed their opportunity and one SBD was dispatched to the target. The assembled and anxious army watchers, including many of the regiment's top brass, had a grandstand view of the attack as they were located on one side of the valley on a high cliff. Visibility was perfect as the Dauntless dived in, etched against the brilliant blue sky, and released its single bomb. It hit, right on target, the enemy detachment. Colonel Rees, suitably impressed, radioed the go-ahead for the plane to drop its main under-belly bomb and its other wing bomb also.

In acknowledgement, the Marine pilot pulled his Dauntless up to regain sufficient altitude, which took some twenty minutes. Meanwhile the rest of the seven SBDs stooged around overhead awaiting their chance. The second dive-bombing run was even more precise and both bombs landed right in among the Japanese. From that moment on, 1 Regiment, anyway, was sold on the Marine flyers and permission was given immediately for the rest of the squadron to join in. Of the 27 bombs that they dropped the furthest off-target was 30 yards away.

Colonel Rees now became an enthusiastic exponent of dive-bombing, according to an eyewitness, McConaughy, so much so that 1 Regiment was to have a permanent stand-by daily requirement of nine flights a day, each of nine SDBs, for the rest of the campaign.

This sortie also confirmed the flexibility of the radio organisation that enabled the army commander, the ALP and the squadron commander in the air to co-operate down to the individual bomb drop. The range of the communications net almost proved its worth, until the air waves became swamped with Allied chatter as the campaign wore on. When the VHF channels became too jammed solid with army aircraft signals, the Marines switched over to MHF.

The Japanese had not been caught completely flat-footed or in disarray by the Lingayen landings – after all, they had themselves invaded the same spot four years before and so did not really expect the American troops to come ashore in Manila Bay. Their plan was to concentrate the bulk of the 250,000-strong 14 Army inland, in three groups, and to restrict the US advance to the plain where they could counter-attack the Americans to good effect. But, like Rommel in Normandy, they had not realised how much command of the air would dictate movement on the ground.

The construction crews got quickly to work and two airstrips were already in operation on Mindoro from 23 December. As a result, when the Japanese tried to switch their divisions to oppose the Americans on Luzon they found their columns dive-bombed off the roads north of the capital and into the dubious sanctuary of the jungle where Filipino guerrillas, loyal to the US, awaited them. Totally confused, their whole defence organisation dissolved under the hail of bombs, among the casualties being the only armoured division the defending General, Tomoyuki Yamsahita, possessed. By 27 January all six airfields at the massive Clark air base had been liberated and the capital finally fell after three weeks' fighting on 23 February. In all of these operations the MAW1 played its full part.

Another personal recollection of how the army became convinced of the merits of dive-bombing was recounted by a historian of the US 24 Regiment. One trooper had become cut off from his comrades and isolated by Japanese patrons:

> It was quiet for a long time. Dive-bombers woke me up next morning. Plane after plane drove into the Nip positions. They dropped napalm and high-explosive bombs all around me. I was covered with dirt and leaves by the explosions and I guess that helped to hide me. The Japs were excited and afraid and they ran all around my position. Maybe they thought I was dead. Maybe they were too busy getting out of there to care. Most of them were killed by the bombs or by the bullets when the planes came back.

During February 1945 the Marine Dauntless units flew no less than 4000 combat sorties. Despite the abundance of Japanese heavy and light AA-guns all over the island their losses were sparse, only three Marine SBD flyers being killed in this period. Of aerial opposition there was none, the last Japanese fighters had long since been shot out of the sky or bombed on the runway, or expended in a suicide dive against the massed US fleets off the beachheads.

In spite of all they had done, and even though the commanders and men on the ground were won over completely, the feeling grew that the Commander-in-Chief was deliberately keeping the Marine dive-bomber wing under-employed. Indeed Admiral 'Bull' Hålsey, never one to mince words, and whose own carrier-borne dive-bombers had been attacking the remnants of the Japanese fleet continuously from Indo-China to Tokyo Bay was forced to make a written comment on just this fact. He told MacArthur bluntly that Army Air Force General Kennedy, when not keeping the 1 Marine Air Group idle, 'was assigning it to missions far below its capacity'. In the upper echelons of the US Army Air Force nothing seemed to have changed since Nadzab.

Despite this negative attitude, the Marine Corps dive-bomber wing continued to apply its perfected technique of close-support for the rest of the Luzon campaign whenever it was allowed. The missions in support of the army continued until the last one was carried out on 14 April 1945. However some units had already shifted to a new area of combat, with the plans to retake most of the southern Philippines. From March 1945 SBDs were flying yet further dive-bomber missions.

The first of these was in support of 41 Division whose own main task was to clear the Sulu Archipelago, and to facilitate this the American troops waded ashore on the south-eastern tip of Mindanao on 21 March to take the Zamboanga peninsula. It took a fortnight's hard fighting for them to get a decent foothold there, but with dive-bomber support from the Marine Air Wing Sirawai fell on 21 March. They then turned their attention to the chain of islands that spanned the northern end of the Celebes Sea from the Philippines to Borneo. In the centre of this chain was the island of Jolo and 163 RCT went ashore there on 9 April to find it was held by 4000 resolute Japanese troops. The fighting, grim and dour, continued for three weeks before the main area of the island was cleared, even so certain units held out until July. The SBDs were in continual demand to break strong points of resistance during this bloody and not widely known episode.

Finally came Cebu, in the central group of the Philippines, guarding the south-west approach to the vital supply route of the Visayan Sea. Here Marine veterans joined hands with army veterans; for the American Division assigned to take Cebu was formed from divisions that had fought at Guadalcanal and Bougainville. They knew each other well and worked well together. The division landed close to Cebu City on 26 March and ran immediately into formidable defences which stopped it dead. Even the beaches were mined. Two weeks hard fighting followed, but some Japanese units were still resisting in June 1945. The bulk of the Allied dive-bombing missions were carried out in support of ground units' but some were highly specialised missions to bring air firepower to Filipino guerilla units. These missions continued until the end of the war.

The Dauntless bombers were now reaching the end of their combat life. One of MAG24's dive-bomber squadrons, VMSB 244, had its Dauntless mounts replaced by SB–2C Helldivers towards the end of May. The other two, VMSB 133 and 241, were de-commissioned on 16 July, near the end of the fighting. Finally, on 1 August 1945, the four SBD squadrons that made up MAG 32 reached the end of their operational tour too and prepared for their return home two weeks later.

It was the end of an era, but the Marine SBD pilots had picked up the proud traditions of 'Rusty' Rowell and his companions in Nicaragua all those years before, and had honed the weapon to perfection and demonstrated its efficiency. Their work in the Philippines campaign laid the foundations of the future role of the US Marine Corps Aviation. The full significance was that, for the first time during the Second World War, they were able to demonstrate the Americans' whole concept of close-support as it is understood at this present day – that is, in assisting large numbers of ground troops.

Although Marine aviators had in other battles, like those at Guadalcanal and Bougainville and, later, Okinawa, utilised certain facets of the doctrine, the real test of the adaptability of close air-support was manifested in the Philippines campaign. As one Marine historian recorded: 'This employment was a notable milestone in the formulation of Marine aviation's post-war mission.'

While the Marines had been earning fresh laurels ashore their navy counterparts aboard Halsey's great carrier fleet had finished with jungle warfare. Ahead of them and also of the Marine Corsair squadrons, lay Okinawa, Iwo Jima and Japan herself. No lush vegetation here, but the same determined foe.

The carrier pilots in their Helldiver did, however, obtain one final glimpse of the jungle-covered slopes before the war zone moved further north.

Halsey had taken his 11 aircraft carriers, six battleships, 13 cruisers and four dozen destroyers right into the South China Sea. This bold move, with Japanese bases on all sides of him, was made with impunity, and on 12 January 1945 Operation GRATITUDE was conducted when almost 500 naval aircraft of Task Force 58 struck at the southern provincial capital and river port of Sanyon in French Indo-China. Four large Japanese transports, two oil tankers and the Vichy-French manned cruiser *Lamotte-Picquet*, which was suspected of being pro-Japanese, were sunk outright in the harbour. Also picked out by the dive-bombers were the massive oil storage tank complexes of Caltex and Shell on the foreshore which were heavily and accurately hit.

The manager of Caltex was ruefully able to confirm after the war just how precise and efficient these dive-bombing attacks were because, in 1947, he was still trying to get them re-started and repaired. His verdict set the seal on the work of the jungle dive-bombers in the Far Eastern campaigns of the Second World War: 'Very accurate bombing – too accurate.'

Despite the coming of peace the jungles of Indo-China were not long to be without the sound of dive-bombers roaring into their attack dives. The throaty bellows of Dauntless and Helldiver re-appeared there before long, but their aircrews would no longer be American, but French. Later still a new generation of young US dive-bomber pilots, flying Douglas Skyraiders, saw similar combat and carried out equally proficient close support for their hard-pressed companions on the ground. But that is another story.

EPILOGUE

In the history of military aviation the battles and achievements of the jungle dive-bomber squadrons have often been as ignored and forgotten as the campaigns themselves. Comments on such events as, for example, the removal of the Australian Vengeance squadrons from Nadzab and their replacement by fighter-bombers have often been made to the effect that 'the resulting loss of accuracy could be accepted'. But what the superior point was in flying faster to the target area while carrying a smaller bomb load, and then missing the target, is not explained by such comments.

The precision and skill of the dive-bombing method, or the later 'lob' method of attack where the bomb was released on the upward movement of the aircraft after the pull-out, and its clear superiority over most other means of air attack when it came to destroying small and well-hidden targets in difficult country, was proven over and over again in the Asian jungle campaigns. Yet the men who achieved these excellent results, for such economy of effort and comparatively small loss, were but a handful of pilots who have been forgotten in the overwhelming mass of the heavy- and medium-bomber fleets that were pounding both Europe and Asia by 1945.

But even the roar of such air fleets and the championing of them by those who back the policy of mass-area bombing paled into insignificance beside the dropping of the atomic bombs on Hiroshima and Nagasaki. With these and the V2 rocket weapon, the huge, costly and largely ineffective armadas of four-engined bombers were rendered as obsolete as the bow and arrow, the musket and the battleship (although ironically, the latter weapons system has survived its often predicted demise at the hands of the heavy bomber and has re-appeared in full fighting trim in the late 1980s as good as ever).

The famous German dive-bomber ace, Hans Ulrich Rudel,

identified perfectly the common wartime and post-war Allied misunderstanding about precision dive-bombing and its effects when he described his debriefing after the war by a succession of American and British air force intelligence officers:

> I soon perceive that we have contrary ideas. This is not surprising seeing that I have flown most of my operational flights with aircraft of very inferior speed and my experience is therefore different from that of the Allies who are inclined to exaggerate the importance of every extra mph, if only as a guarantee of safety. They can hardly believe my total of over 2500 sorties with a slow aircraft, nor are they at all interested to learn the lesson of my experience as they see no life insurance in it. They boast of their rockets which I already know about and which can be fired from the fastest aircraft; they do not like to be told that their accuracy is small in comparison with my cannon.

They know quite differently *now,* of course, but it took a long time for the lessons of the jungle dive-bombers to sink in. Nor were the views of the army on the ground much sought either, at any level, for it was not thought politic for the airmen to consult them. The policy seemed to be to accept the air support we offer you rather than what type of air support would you find most helpful. This is encapsulated concisely in a recent history:

> Heavy bomber attacks employed tactically often turned out to be counter-productive, and ground commanders on both sides remarked in memoirs that they found dive-bombers with their pinpoint accuracy useful, but preferred artillery to heavy high-level bombers, for the latter made such a mess as to create impassable conditions.

In the forty or more years that have elapsed since the final battles described in this book, more and more often it has been the subtle skills of precision and accuracy, of the picking out of specific vital targets and the placing of limited bomb loads to the greatest effect, which has dominated the close-support role of the bitter local wars fought in the jungle zones of the world, rather than the indiscriminate sledge-hammer slaughter advocated between 1919 and 1945. Instead of pouring scorn on aircraft such as the Junkers Ju 87 Stuka, or the Douglas AD Skyraider, it has proved to be such aircraft that have held the

line in French Indo-China or Korea, or Vietnam. And far from
protesting, like one blinkered Air Marshal did in 1941, that the
last thing Britain's defenders wanted in order to repel German
Panzers was, 'dive-bomber aircraft skidding about over Kent
looking for tanks, that is the job of the artillery', now whole
squadrons of NATO close-support aircraft have been built
with just that specific task in mind. It is recognised as a highly
vital role.

The principal school of that long learning had been in the
jungle dive-bomber squadrons of the Second World War, and it
was in the Far East that the lessons – painfully imparted by the
Val, the Vengeance, the Dauntless and the Helldiver, and later
ignored – had to be repeatedly demonstrated again, first by
French Navy dive-bomber pilots, then by US Marine and
Navy flyers.

The first of the post-war applications of close-support dive-
bombing was conducted by the French in what was then their
colonial empire of Indo-China which encompassed the present
nations of Vietnam, Laos and Cambodia.

As early as 1943 the revitalised French Navy Air Service had
requested a delivery of Douglas SBD-5 Dauntless dive-
bombers as part of their re-building programme. It was not
until November 1944, however, that delivery was finally taken
at Agadir, Morocco, of 32 such aircraft. These dive-bombers
were formed into two Air Flotillas, 3B and 4B, and began
training. This was necessarily brief for shortly afterwards they
flew to Cognac in France. Here they undertook numerous
combat missions against German troops and fortresses, particularly Lorient, until the end of the war in Europe.

It had been hoped to use a group aboard an aircraft carrier to
join the American and British Task Forces in the final drive on
Japan in 1945. However, the only French aircraft carrier afloat,
Bearn, was too ancient for this. A replacement vessel was
sought from the Allies but the war in the Pacific terminated
before this could be organised. After the end of the war against
Japan, however, troubles almost immediately broke out in
Indo-China.

Because of this the SBDs did reach the Far East after all,

aboard the escort carrier *Dixmude,* formerly the British *Biter* which was transferred to France on 9 April 1945. She was far from suitable but she was a carrier, more or less, and could be utilised as an aircraft transport. Squadron 3 F B (re-numbered as 3 F) began embarking aboard her shortly afterwards together with ex-British Seafire fighter aircraft. Since some of the Dauntless had always operated from land bases and had fixed wings, not folding, this meant a very tight fit in the small hangars of the *Dixmude.* Nonetheless flying operations from her tiny deck proved feasible with the help of the S B D's massive and effective dive-flaps.

The French Indo-China war had started on 9 December 1946. *Dixmude,* with her dive-bomber squadron, had already sailed for that theatre of war and she landed them in the north of Indo-China during February 1947. Soon the nine S B Ds of 3 F Squadron were urgently in demand to fight the growing strength of the Communist columns. Because of the limited space aboard the small carrier coupled with the lack of powerful catapults for launching aboard this type of ship and the fact that her maximum speed of 16.5 knots was too slow to permit the S B Ds to unstick from her deck very easily, 3F Squadron mainly operated during the next three years from shore airfields at Tonkin.

Dixmude herself returned to Toulon on 14 April 1947 for a refit and to embark the remainder of the aircraft. On 20 October she again sailed for Indo-China with 4F Squadron (ex 4FB) duly embarked under the command of Lieutenant de Vaisseau Mellet. Three of these aircraft were also sent to Tonkin, the other six to Cochin China. At the end of November 1947 they took part in the first battles in Central Anam and afterwards participated in the battle of Tan Son Nhut, in the Plain of Jars campaign.

These two units kept up the tradition of strikes and attacks in the Red River area. However they were already ageing and this period of intensive combat duty wore them out completely. They flew their last combat sorties on 26 and 29 March 1948. By July 1949 they had to be replaced by fresh purchases of American dive-bombers. Meanwhile a larger aircraft carrier had been purchased to replace *Dixmude*. This was the light carrier *Arromanches* (ex-British *Colossus*).

On 29 November 1948 *Arromanches* arrived off Cape Saint Jacques, and disembarked, among other aircraft, ten more SBD-5s of 4F, Squadron commanded by Lieutenant de Vaisseau Rollin, to join 3F. Its operational debut was on 11 December 1948, but co-operation between the Aeronavale and the troops on the ground was very difficult because of uncertainty over how best to employ such tactics. It had taken an intensive effort by the US Marine Corps to achieve this even when concentrating solely on just that one aspect, and with their vast resources of aircraft, men and radios. The small number of French SBDs could not match this, nor did the French army have much experience either of working such tactics to the best effect.

Operating from a mobile base the few SBDs had to be on call against a mobile and fleeting enemy and co-ordination was always difficult to achieve. 4F Squadron, operating mainly in the Tonkin region, suffered from many breakdowns as their age crept up on them, the use of such old machines making normal operational hazards yet more dangerous for their aircrew.

After 56 such combat missions, during which they clocked up 300 hours combat flying time, these SBDs finally returned to France aboard *Arromanches* on 5 January 1949. The major loss, in June, had been the death in a flying accident of Lieutenant Rollin himself.

Replacements later took their place on the firing line, these being the AB–2C–5 Helldivers bought in 1950. (Batches of the same mark also served in the jungle with the Royal Thai Air Force from 1953 to 1955.) Four dozen of these dive-bombers were purchased in an initial order, forming two new Air Flotillas, 3F and 9F. It was the latter that saw the first war service. On 9 April 1951 this unit, which had been equipped with Supermarine Walrus and Dornier 9FTr amphibians at Sartrouville flew to Hyères to be re-equipped with the dive-bombers. When *Arromanches* returned to Indo-China waters towards the end of 1942 it was with 9F Flotilla's dive-bombers. When they arrived, they found work a-plenty.

The first great Communist offensive had erupted out of the highlands towards the end of 1950. It came up against French airpower and, even in its limited form, they had not liked what they found. The French were operating close to the sea and to their air bases, and could use what limited aircraft they had to good effect against the massed enemy columns. An early example occurred on 22 December 1950, when a Vietminh column was observed near to the north coast of Along Bay, near Tien Yen. It could threaten the vital Red River delta and a French paratroop regiment was sent to disperse it. Direct support was given by aircraft and, for the first time in Indo-China, liberal use was made of napalm. Each aircraft had wing tanks filled with jellied petroleum which they dropped like bombs. On impact the tanks detonated in a sheet of fire. Lumps of sticky fire cascaded over a wide area and decimated large numbers of the enemy.

This violent revelation of the effect of close air support was a bitter lesson for the peasant army. Even disciplined units were uneasy under the threat of air attack, and often broke when it materialised. This slowed down their movements a great deal and helped the heavily outnumbered French ground forces.

Another significant encounter took place on 16 and 17 January 1951 when a massed assault by two Communist Divisions, 308 and 312, was made against French defensive positions on the Red River, north-east of Hanoi at Vinh Yen. Regardless of losses, wave after wave of infantry flooded forward, was mown down and scattered by automatic fire and immediately replaced by another wave. Such tactics, with the callous disregard for casualties, could easily overrun any position in time but, again, it was the introduction of the French dive-bombers that saved the day. Every available aircraft was thrown into the battle with bombs, machine-guns and napalm. At the end of two days of slaughter some 9000 Vietminh soldiers had been killed, 600 taken prisoner, and 8000 wounded, out of an attacking force of 22,000 men. The assault had been broken.

Initially the Vietminh commander, General Vo Nyguyen Giap, had taken inspiration from his Red Chinese colleagues in the belief that these 'human wave' tactics, as they were currently

being practised with success in Korea, would produce the
same results in Vietnam. It took time for the lesson to sink in.
However, the regiments were re-constructed and thrown into a
new offensive together with the 316 Division and 148 Independ-
ent Regiment in a new assault across the Red River on 14
October 1952. This time they broke through the French defence line after a week's fighting, and threatened to flood south
and engulf the whole region.

At the isolated French airfield of Na-Sen they met a break-
water in the form of a hastily reinforced defensive position, or
'hedgehog', to use German Eastern Front parlance. Against
this, which was centred on the airstrip, into which reinforcements were continuously flown, the waves broke in vain. The
French termed this fortress a Base Aero-Terrestre, an Air-
Land Base. It was well dug-in with mutually supporting defence lines, well laced with automatic weapons. Again mass
attacks resulted in the mass slaughter of the attackers. Giap
returned to guerrilla tactics. The French thought they had
found the answer to jungle fighting. It was a fateful precedent
for both sides.

The Helldivers of 9F Flotilla served faithfully in this theatre
for two years, undertaking a whole variety of missions which
included much true dive-bombing as well as strafing, rocket
and napalm attacks at low level. In total the Flotilla carried out
824 combat sorties which represented some 2000 hours flying
time during which they dropped 1442 tons of bombs and
expended 100,000 rounds of machine-gun ammunition against
Vietminh targets of all kinds. In 1953 they returned to France
and converted to the German Avenger torpedo-bomber. Their
place was taken by 3F Flotilla with a new batch of Helldivers.
With this unit the French Navy dive-bombers were to earn
undying fame at the last big battle of the war where their
reputation for flying lower and more often than their Air Force
companions gained them the highest esteem from the trapped
and doomed Legionnaires.

The siege and fall of Dien Bien Phu in 1954, while not the
actual end of the shooting war, marked the end of the will of the
French nation as a whole to shoulder the burden of resistance

alone after requests for both American (physical) and British (moral) backing had both been turned down by Eisenhower and Churchill respectively. The compromise dividing of Vietnam into two parts, however, did not satisfy the Communists; it merely postponed the inevitable. As soon as they had built up their strength again the North invaded the South just as had happened in Korea. This time the United Nations did nothing so, following the Gulf of Tonkin incident on 2 August 1964, when North Vietnamese torpedo-boats attacked the US destroyer *Maddox* and other ships, the United States retaliated by stepping in to take up the fight which they had encouraged the French to abandon.

Naturally the fastest way to bring succour to the hard-pressed southern forces was through carrier-based airpower; and it was the US 7 Fleet which mounted the first reprisal raid of 5 August. These first strikes were against the bases of the North Vietnamese torpedo-boats which had caused the Tonkin incident, and the attack was conducted by VA–52, a Douglas A1H Skyraider squadron embarked aboard the carrier *Constellation*. These propeller-driven dive-bombers were direct descendants of the Second World War SBD Dauntless, and were also designed by Ed Heinemann. They were supported by another Skyraider unit, VA145, from USS *Ticonderoga*.

Although these first missions were not against jungle targets, that soon changed. South Vietnam had been using these dive-bombers in her own squadrons since 1962. They utilised A1 Skyraiders which had been mothballed since the Korean war. Eventually the Vietnamese Air Force had several squadrons of the 'Spad', with 41 Wing at Da Nang, 74 at Bihn Thuy and 23 at Bien Hoa. The most famous of their Skyraider squadrons was 83 Squadron which was commanded for a time by the South Vietnam premier, Nguyen Gao Ky.

The US Navy was in the process of switching from Skyraiders to the new jet close-support types, the A4C Skyhawk and the A6A Intruder but twelve squadrons of the old dive-bombers still remained with the fleet and they soon began to give a good account of themselves – so much so that even the US Air Force finally became convinced of the value of accuracy

over speed for close-support operations. Accordingly, the
USAF formed two Skyraider squadrons of their own, 603 and
604. One historian wrote:

> As the Navy had learned years ago, the US Air Force would come
> to realise that this particular airplane, with its ability to carry large
> payloads and remain over the target area for long periods of time,
> was the best close ground support aircraft that could be used for the
> type of 'brush fire war' that was being carried on in Vietnam.

Interdiction missions were conducted almost daily against
Vietcong targets in South Vietnam itself but, on 2 March
1965, the Skyraiders took the dive-bomber war direct to the
enemy when targets north of the 17 Parallel at Dong Hoi,
Quang Binh and Vinh Linn were hit for the first time. Bridges,
and road and rail links, were the precision targets the 'Able
Dogs' (AD for Attack Douglas) Skyraider squadrons were sent
against, but in the confused jungle fighting, where ground
troops could be pinned down by an unseen enemy, the ability of
the dive-bomber to linger in the area until the enemy was
spotted, and then deliver an exact and devastating attack, was a
quality which none of the new generation close-support jets
could match.

A good example of their worth and value was demonstrated
during the Battle of Dong Xoai. This was a Special Forces
camp located 50 miles north-east of Saigon. This base was in
grave danger of being overrun by a surprise attack by a huge
enemy force in the blackness of the early hours of 10 June 1965.
The position at first seemed hopeless, but it was resolved by
Navy and VNAF dive-bombers.

A C–47 aircraft equipped with flares was dispatched at once
to the scene of the disaster, followed some time later by a
second. Twenty minutes later two Vietnamese A1Es were
homing in on their lights but were unable to attack because of
the cloud base which was down to 500ft. At 04.30 the two US
Navy A1es also arrived over the target. Their pilots were
Captain Richard Y. Costain and Captain Doyle C. Ruff, and as
they listened to the hard-pressed South Vietnamese troops on
their radio they determined to throw away the rule book and

bring what succour they could before it was too late. What followed next was an example of classic jungle close-support technique.

Flying only by instrument, both pilots took their dive-bombers down into the cloud base and then dived through it to be met by a hail of intense anti-aircraft fire from six automatic cannon and many machine-guns. Despite this they homed their Skyraiders on to the light of the burning strongpoint and carried out their attacks, each 'Spad' unloading two dozen 260-lb fragmentation bombs on the target area. Costain then made two dive-bombing runs from 5000ft down to 1000ft, directed by a Forward Air Controller, and released his main ordnance right on to the enemy main positions.

The Vietcong troops were pouring over the walls at this time and the defenders radioed that this presented a perfect target for 20mm cannon fire. Costain and Ruff responded immediately, starting their strafing runs from under 500ft and between them they emptied 15,000 rounds of cannon shells into the massed ranks of the Communist assault units. Despite the intensity of the return fire both aircraft survived, although Costain's Skyraider took three direct hits, two of them in his engine, while Ruff, pulling 7Gs in his attack dive, became disoriented and almost hit the ground. Their prompt action caused dismay among the Vietcong regiment, however, and made it pause at a critical juncture.

With the arrival of first light more dive-bomber sorties began to arrive over the target zone, no less than two dozen A1Hs and 35 A1Es joining with other aircraft in a non-stop assault on the enemy. By 07.45 the Allied troops had regained part of the compound and were calling for more strikes on the remaining enemy positions. Again it was the diver-bombers which responded, and eight A1Es made concentrated attacks between 06.00 and 08.00 on a schoolhouse occupied by the Vietcong.

Meanwhile, under cover of both Air Force and VNAF Skyraiders, relief forces were flown in and, by 09.40, had begun to counter-attack the enemy. One of the dive-bomber pilots, Major Oscar Manterer, was on his first combat mission in Vietnam. He had not even had training time to practise any type

of attack, day or night, nor was he familiar with the multiple
bomb racks on the A1E. When he made his initial bombing run
he went straight down to 1000ft with his navigation lights full
on, as the master switch had failed to work, before pulling out.
He survived this to make a second dive on an enemy gun
position which he hit with four 100-lb GP bombs. still with his
lights ablaze.

Another Skyraider pilot turned a blind eye to standing
instructions later that same day. Although the overcast remained stubbornly thick from 4000ft down to 800ft Captain
Richard D. Head led his three A1Es down through it in fine
disregard and they planted their 260-lb fragmentation bombs
on the enemy from 800ft. Further strikes followed and hits were
taken by all three dive-bombers, but they survived to return
safely to their base. Such strikes continued all day.

Under cover of darkness the following night, the enemy
renewed his offensive on Dong Xoai but even this failed to
protect them for two A1Es provided continual support until
21.00 when the enemy broke off their assault in frustration.
A1Es stayed on the job all night just in case. Early on 11 June 19
A1Es and 14 A1Hs joined in mass strikes against the remnants
of the enemy force, adding rockets to their bomb and machine-
gun fire. In all some 45 tons of bombs and 40 tons of incendiaries plus 20,000 rounds of 20mm cannon shell completed the
rout of the Communist force. Between 300 and 400 Vietcong
dead were later counted on the ground; most of the wounded,
in true guerrilla style, were carried away by their friends to die
in hidden locations.

The true worth of the jungle dive-bomber squadrons was
given glowing tribute by General William C. Westmoreland,
the Commander-in-Chief of US forces in Vietnam:

> The performance of your strike pilots in providing close air support
> for the Dong Xoai 9–11 June operations was singularly outstand-
> ing. Working under adverse weather conditions, your pilots dis-
> played true professionalism and delivered their weapons with
> precision. They, in fact, turned the tide of the battle.

Such a statement, taken along with those of General Wavell

in Burma, Generalissimo Chiang Kai-shek in China, the 'Coastwatchers' in the Solomons, General Mudge in the Philippines, the Foreign Legion in Dien Bien Phu and countless other grateful soldiers in a thousand or more anonymous, desperate fights, are the true and valid indications of the worth of the dive-bomber in jungle warfare.

However with the latest technology, including the introduction of radar-guided (SMART) bombs, it was only a matter of time before the last 'Spads' were phased out. Many veteran aircrew were not overkeen to change over to the new generation jets, however, and the troops on the ground were even more reluctant to see the friendly angular shape vanish from their limited horizons. They had come to have the same sort of affection for them as the German troopers in the Second World War had for the ever-reliable Stuka on the Eastern Front.

One of the last successful land operations, in which the roar of the dive-bomber was heard over the Asian jungles, was almost a re-run of the battle for Dien Bien Phu, but with a happier outcome. This was the battle of Khe Sanh, a US Marine Corps base on a strategic hill in north-west South Vietnam. Here, starting in January 1968 at the time of the infamous 'Tet' offensive, the human-wave tactics employed by Giap were utilised once more against an isolated and surrounded US 26 Marines garrison. Once again the strongpoint would have to rely on air protection, and this time it received it in full measure. This was the principal difference between Operation SCOTLAND and the siege of Dien Bien Phu. Among the support aircraft directed to the enemy formations by the Forward Air Controllers (FAC) under the sophisticated defence plan (coded as Operation NIAGARA), were the old 'Spads'. VNAG Skyraiders were prominent in supporting the Marines in their long and bitter struggle. But as the more detailed official Marine Corps account states:

> During the day, the air around Khe Sanh was filled with the high-pitched shriek of jet engines: Marine, Navy and Air Force F4 Phantoms; Marine and Navy A6 Intruders, A4 Skyhawks and F8 Crusaders; Air Force F-105 Thunderchiefs and F100 Super Sabres. In addition to the jets, the South Vietnamese prop-driven

A1 Skyraider, a rugged attack aircraft of Korean War vintage, was in evidence. At times the sky overhead resembled a giant beehive.

So passed the famous old Skyraider and with it a whole epoch of air warfare in which it was the bravery and skill of the individual pilot or aircrew that mattered more than all the technological resource and theory that is now required by modern flying.

SOURCES

Air Force Historical Division: *The Army Air Forces in World War II: Volume Four – The Pacific: Guadalcanal to Saipan; August 1942 to July 1944*, ed. Wesley Frank Craven & James Lea Cate, University of Chicago Press, Chicago, 1967.

Air Force Historical Division: Group History 311 Fighter Bomber Group, Army Air Forces, APO 487, dated 7 November 1943, dated 7 December 1943. DIR 5200.9. APO487, dated 9 January 1944, dated 5 February 1944, dated 5 March 1944, dated 5 April 1944, dated 5 May 1944, dated 5 June 1944, dated 5 July 1944 (copies in author's collection).

Air Force Historical Division: 528 Fighter Bomber Squadron, Army Air Forces APO 467, dated 5 November 1943, dated 4 January 1944, dated 2 February 1944 (copies in author's collection).

Air Force Historical Division: 529 Fighter Bomber Squadron, Army Air Forces APO 487, dated 5 November 1943, dated 4 January 1944, dated 2 February 1944 (copies in author's collection).

Air Force Historical Division: 530 Fighter Bomber Squadron, Army Air Force APO 490, dated 31 December 1943, dated 31 January 1944 (copies in author's collection).

Air Force Historical Division: 311 Fighter Group, Office of the Intelligence Officer, APO 210, dated 3 April 1944, dated 8 December 1944. GP–311–H1 July 1943–November 1944 Declassified DOD Directive 5200.9., dated 27 September 1958 (copies in author's collection).

Air Command New Georgia: *Daily Intelligence Summaries*, 29 June 1943 to 13 August 1943; *Special Action Report*, 1944 (US Army Air Force Historical Section (photocopies in author's collection).

Anon: *Okinawa – Final Stepping Stone* (Historical Branch HQ, USMC, Washington DC, January 1969 (photocopy in author's collection).

Anon: *Action Report Commander Air Group 18 for period 12–14 September 1944*, US Navy Historical Records Division, Washington Navy Yard, DC, 91018, September 1944 (photocopy in author's collection).

Anon: *Bombing Squadron Six (VB–6), 15 March 1943–29 October 1943* (US Navy Historical Records Division, Washington DC, 1943 (photocopy in author's collection).

Boyington, Col. Gregory 'Pappy', USMC: *Baa Baa Black Sheep*, Putnam, London, 1958.

Chassin, General L.M.: *Aviation Indochine*, Amiot-Dumont, Paris, 1954.

Gill, Arthur M., RAF: Flying Log Book, 1942–63 (on extended loan to author).

Hinkle, Stacy C.: *Wings and Saddles: The Air and Cavalry Punitive Expedition of 1919*, Southwest Studies, Monograph No 19, University of Texas at El Paso, 1974.

Hinkle, Stacy C. *Wings over the Border; the Army Air Service Armed Patrol of the United States–Mexico Border 1919–1921* (Southwest Studies, Monograph No 26, University of Texas at El Paso, 1970)).

Jackson, B.R., *Douglas Skyraider*, Aero Publications, Fallbrook, California, 1969.

Jensen, Lieutenant Oliver, USNR: *Carrier War*, Simon & Schuster, New York, 1945.

Limbrick, George A.: Flying Log Book, 1942–6. (on extended loan to author).

McInnes, 'Red'. Flying Log Book, 1941–5, (on extended loan to author).

Matheson, Col. Bruce J., USMC 'The Corsair and its Contributions', *Air and Space Museum Inducts*, May 1981, p. 59 (copy in author's collection).

Molesworth, Carl and Moseley, H. Stephens, MD: *Fighter Operations of the Chinese–American Composite Wing*, Research Project 8010, American Aviation Historical Society Journal, no 127, no 4, Winter 1982, Santa Ana, Ca (copy in author's collection).

Naval Analysis Division, Marshalls-Gilberts-New Britain Party: *The Allied Campaign against Rabaul*, US Strategic Bombing Survey (Pacific), 1946 (photocopies in author's collection).

Noel, Jean: Curtiss SB2C–5 Helldiver' (article, *AviMag*, 1963).

Odgers, George: *Air War against Japan, 1943–1945*, Australian War Memorial, Camberra, 1957.

Okumiyra, Masatake, and Horikoshi, Jiro: *Zero!: The Story of the Japanese Navy Air Force, 1937–1945*, Cassell, London, 1957.

Olds, Robert: *Helldiver Squadron*, Dodd Mead, New York, 1945.

Patou, Le Capitaine de Vaisseau. *Group Porte Avions d'Extreme Orient: Rapport d'Operations, Periode du 26 Decembre 1953 au 2 Juin 1954* (various reports of this period, 250 pages, 1954, photocopies in author's collection).

Piper, Robert Kendall: 'Dive-Bomber "Blow-Ins" ', article in *Australian Post*, 2 January 1986 (photocopy in author's collection, courtesy of Bob Piper).

RAAF Historical Section: Narrative Reports, Various Squadrons, Nadzab (Intelligence Office Reports, RAAF, Nadzab, 1944 (photocopies in author's collection).

Royal Air Force: Operational Log No 168 Wing, RAF, India, 1942–1944, RAF, 1944, AIR 26v246 7965 (photocopy in author's collection).

Ritchie, Donald A. RAAF: Flying Log Book, 1942–6 (on extended loan to author).

RNZAF Historical Branch. Operational Room Log, 25 Dive Bomber Squadron, RNZAF, AIR 160v3, 1944 (photocopy in author's collection).

RNZAF Historical Branch. Operational Log Book, 25 Dive Bomber Squadron, Feb–April 1944 AIR 160v7, 1944 (photocopy in author's collection).

Rudel, Hans Ulrich. *Stuka Pilot*, Euphorion, Dublin, 1952.

Sakai, Saburo: *Samarai*, William Kimber, London, 1959.

Sams, Kenneth: 'Tactical Air Support: Balancing the Scales in Vietnam', *Air Force*, Washington DC, August 1965.

Santelli, James S.: *Marines in the Recapture of the Philippines*, Historical Branch HQ, USMC, Washington DC, March 1969 (photocopy in author's collection).

SEAC Air Command. *Dive-Bombing: An Introduction*. Air Command, S.E. Asia Tactical Memorandum No 5, 1 December 1943 (AIR 24v1376–5289).

Shaw, Henry I, jnr., and Kane, Maj. Douglas T., USMC: *Isolation of Rabaul: History of US Marine Corps Operations in World War II*,

Volume II, Historical Branch, US Marine Corps HG, Washington DC, 1963 (photocopies in author's collection).

Sherrod, Robert: *History of Marine Corps Aviation in World War II*, Combat Forces Press, Washington DC, 1952.

Stafford, Cdr Wdward P. USN: *The Big E*, Random House, New York, 1974.

Stokesbury, James L.: *A Short History of Air Power*, Robert Hale, London, 1986.

Strike Command Intelligence Section. War Diary Strike Command, 2 April 1943–19 November 1943. Strike Command Intelligence, 1944, various reports; (photocopies in author's collection).

Strike Command Intelligence Section: Summary of SBD Operations, 1–31 August 1943, Henderson Field, Guadalcanal (Lt. Weston J. Donehower) (photocopies in author's collection).

US Marine Corps: *The Battle for Khe Sanh*. Official, Washington DC (copy in author's collection).

US Strategic Bombing Survey: Interrogations of Japanese Officers, Naval Analysis Division, Washington DC, 1945, US Naval Archives (photocopies in author's collection).

Walton, Col. Frank E., USMC: 'Corsair', *Air and Space Museum Inducts*, May 1981, p. 59.

Whelan, Russell: *The Flying Tigers*, Macdonald, London, 1944.

INDEX

Aaron Ward, destroyer, 44
Admiralty Islands, 66
Aichi D-3A 'Val', 20, 34, 40, 41, 44, 51
Air Liaison Parties, 148, 152
Air Support, 146
Alabama, battleship, 128
Alexander, Capt George W., 94
Alexishafen, 59, 64, 66
American Volunteer Group, 22, 23, 26, 29, 101, 103
Arnold, General 'Hap', 19, 92, 145
Arromanches, light carrier, 164
Arunta, destroyer, 41
Avenger, Grumman TBP/TBM, 108, 113, 115, 119–22, 133, 134, 141

Bailey, F/Sgt, 117
Baisden, Charlie, 28
Baldwin, Air Marshal, 91
Banshee, 21
Baraulu, Island, 40
Barket, F/O, 107
Bau Island, 40
Bearn, aircraft carrier, 162
Bell, F.D., 119
Bellatrix, troop transport, 43
Belleau Wood, light carrier, 128
Bennett, Lt-Col T. Alan, 103
Betty bomber, 37, 38
Bible Hill, 149
Bien Hoa, 167
Birmingham, cruiser, 51
Bishop, Lou, 28
Biter, escort carrier, 163
Blackburn, F/Lt, 77, 87
Blenheim, 18–19, 22, 72
Boden, F/Sgt, 114
Bogan, Rear-Admiral Gerald F., 128, 131
Bond, Charlie, 27
Bonin Islands, 123, 129
Bougainville, 37, 40, 53, 106, 109, 110, 111, 114, 116, 122, 123, 125, 150, 151
Bourke, Brig-Gen T.E., 153
Boyington, 25

Brahmaputra Valley, 93, 94
Brazil, transport, 93
Brereton, Maj-Gen Lewis H., 5, 26
Brewster 339, 21
Brewster SB2A Buccaneer, 17, 145
Brewster Buffalo, 18
Brown, F/O L.H.F., 124
Brownson, destroyer, 53
Bugner, Lt Leo, 104
Buin, 35, 40, 47, 48, 49
Buka, 35, 37, 124
Bumi River, 57
Buna, 21, 145
Bunker Hill, 51, 128, 131
Burma Road, 22, 24, 27
Burnell, F/O N.G., 65

Cabot, light carrier, 128
Cadiz, 132
Calhoun, destroyer-transport, 43
Calvert, Brig 'Mike', 99
Cam's Saddle, 61
Cape Friendship, 122
Cape Gloucester, 53
Cape Saint Jacques, 164
Carmichael, Master-Sgt E.W., 107
Caroline Island, 135
Cebu, 157
Celebes, 127
Celebes Sea, 157
Celeno, transport, 47
Chandler, Lt-Col Charles G. jnr, 92, 94
Chase, Brig William C., 153
Chennault, Gen Clair Lee, 22–7, 29, 31, 101
Chiang Kai-shek, Gen, 22, 26, 90, 171
Chiang Kai-shek, Madame, 25, 31
Chichi Jima, 129
China Air Task Force, 101, 103
Chinese/American Composite Wing (CACW), 103, 104
Churchill, (Sir) Winston, 167
Clark air base, 156
Cochran, Col Philip, 91
Constellation, aircraft carrier, 167

Conyngham, destroyer, 45
Cook Reef, 108
Coral Sea, 33, battle of, 34, 54
Cornwall, cruiser, 20
Corsair, Chance Vought, 40, 149, 151
Costain, Capt Richard Y., 168–9
Cowpens, light carrier, 128
Cray, PO G.H., 119
Crevoisier, F.P., 133

Dakota, 73, 80, 94, 98
Dalu Valley, 95
Dauntless, Douglas SBD, 19, 21 107, 111, 112, 115, 117–24, 128, 145, 149, 155, 156, 158, 159, 162, 163
Davies, Col S., 57
Davison, Rear-Admiral Ralph E., 128
De Haven, destroyer, 44
De Havilland Aircraft Manufacturing Co, 3–4
de Lange, S/Ldr (later Air Cmdr) T.J. McL., 105, 110
DH-4, 3, 4–7
Dien Bien Phu, 2, 166, 171
Digbol Refinery, 94
Dill, Gen Sir John, 17
Dive-bombing, early development of, 3–12
Dixmude, escort carrier, 163
Dong Hoi, 168
Dong Xoai, Battle of, 168, 170
Dorsetshire, cruiser, 20
Douhet, Gen, 1
Drayton, destroyer, 53
Duke of York islands, 35

Edwards, F/Lt J.W., 122
Eisenhower, Gen 167
Elephant bridge, 86
Empress Augusta Bay, 106, 109, 111
Enterprise, aircraft carrier, 37, 128, 129, 139, 140
Espiritu Santo, 108
Essex, aircraft carrier, 51, 128

Feland, Brig-Gen, 8
Feldt, Cdr Eric, 148
Ferguson, Capt Bob, 104
Finschafen, 54, 56, 57
Fitzwater, S/Ldr G.M., 124
Floyd, Maj, 10
Flying Tigers, 22, 23, 29
Fort Hertz valley, 95
Foshee, Ben C., 27
Franklin, cruiser, 128, 129, 139, 141

French Navy Air Service, 162
Fuller, troop transport, 43
Fyffe, Air Cmdr E.G., 56, 59, 60

Gabrielson, PO, 81–2
Galahad Force, 98
Gazelle Peninsula, 35
Gehres, Capt, 142
Genga, WO Ota, 42
George F. Elliott, troop transport, 39
Gerber, Gen Vo Nyguyen, 165
Gibbs, Dennis, 83
Gibson, Lt-Cdr George Davis 'Hoot', 130
Gili Gili, 41
Gill, S/Ldr Arthur M., 72–88, 91
Glover, Gen, 83
Gori River Bridge, 62, 63
Graham, FO, 109, 114
Gray, F/Sgt, 117
Green Island, 112, 115, 119, 123
Grumman F-4F, 37
Guadalcanal, 33–53, 147

Halsey, Admiral William F. 'Bull', 50, 111, 128, 136–8, 141, 156, 158–9
Hamp fighter, 117, 132, 134
Hansa Bay, 64
Hap fighter, 94
Hardin, Lt Jim, 142
Harvey Bay, 44
Hatfield, Capt, 9
Hawk, 24, 31
Hawk 81A, 26
Hawke, F/Lt, 77
Hawker Hurricane, 18, 22, 23
Hayward, Tom, 28
Head, Capt Richard D., 170
Heinemann, Ed, 167
Hellcat, 129, 131, 132, 141
Helldiver, 51, 128–35, 139–41, 145, 151, 158, 159, 164, 166
Henderson Field, 36, 42, 43, 45, 46, 48, 114, 147
Hermes, aircraft carrier, 20
Hill, David 'Tex', 23, 28, 29, 101, 102
Hoffman, Roy, 26, 28
Honey, S/Ldr Barton, 56, 60, 61
Horikoshi, Jiro, 37, 53
Hornbeak, Ensign Les, 140
Hornet II, fleet carrier, 127
Hospital Ridge, 121
Howard, FO J., 30, 114
Hudson bomber, 34
Hughes, Lt, 130
Hukawng Valley, 94

Hunter, FO Ian G., 57
Huon Gulf, 56
Huon Peninsula, 60

ICHIGO offensive, 104
Ichiki, Col, 39
Imphal, 91, 98
Independence, aircraft carrier, 51, 128
Indiana, battleship, 128
Intrepid, aircraft carrier, 128, 131, 133
Intruder, 167
Invader A36-A ('Apache'), 90–104, 145
Iowa, battleship, 128
Ironbottom Sound, 38
Irrawaddy river, 98
Iwo Jima, 129

Japanese Naval Air Corps, 16, 20, 33
Japanese Navy, 13, 16, 19
Jensen, Lt Oliver, 51
John Penn, transport, 43
Johns, F/Lt, 78
Johnson, F/Lt T.R.F., 121
Johnstone, Doug, 55
Jones, Col Clayton B., 150
Jones, Tom, 28
'Judy' dive-bomber, 139, 142
Junkers Ju 87 'Stuka', 19, 144, 147, 151, 161, 177

Kanawha, oil tanker, 44
Kate, 51
Kavieng, 111
Kawaguchi, Gen, 43
Kawasaki Ki48, 22
Keech, WO Q.A., 78
Kelly, Lt-Col John R., 92
Kenda, Lt-Gen, 106, 109
Kennedy, Gen George C., 50, 56, 59, 157
Keravia Bay, 113
Kittyhawk, 21, 23, 26, 28, 30, 65, 69, 101, 102
Kline, Rip, 51
Koga, Admiral, 53
Kohima, 91
Kokoda Trail, 41
Kolombangara Island, 48
Krantz, 133
Kumbhirgram, 80
Kunming, 25, 27
Kurum, 66
Kusaka, Vice-Admiral Jinichi, 43, 116
Kweilin, 104
Ky, Nguyen Gao, 167

Lae, 54, 56, 57, 145
Lakunai, 34, 35, 36, 49, 112, 119, 120, 121, 124
Lambeti Plantation, 149
Lamotte-Picquet, cruiser, 159
Lamson, destroyer, 53
Laner, Ensign D., 133
Lang, destroyer, 40
Langemak Bay, 58
Langley II, light carrier, 128
Lankford, 133
Laughlin, Lind (C.H.) jnr, 28
Lawlor, Frank, 28
Le-U, 79, 87
Lee, Vice-Admiral Willis A., 128
Legaspi Field, 140
Lentaigne, Maj-Gen 'Joe', 98, 99
Lewis, F/Lt Richard R., 57, 63–5
Lexington II, aircraft carrier, 128
Leyte Gulf, Battle of, 141
Liberator bomber, 94
Lily, 134
Lingayen, 153, 155
Little, Bob, 28, 103
Lowood, 59, 60
LST66, 53
LST202, 53
LST339, 45
LST340, 45
LST471, 45
LST473, 45
Lunga Point, 43
Lunga Roads, 44
Luzon, 139, 153, 156, 157

Mabalacat East, 139
McAllister, FO C., 65
MacArthur, Gen Douglas, 50, 54, 66, 105, 127
McCain, Rear-Admiral J.S., 127
McCaughey's Knoll, 61
McClure, Maj-Gen, 48
McCutcheon, Lt-Col Keith B., 150, 151
McDonald, F/Sgt, F.G., 121
McLellan-Symonds, FO, 114
McNab, F/Lt P.R., 118
McPherson, Cyril, 55, 69
Mactan Island, 135
Madang, 54, 59, 61, 62, 65, 66
Maddox, destroyer, 167
Main, F/Sgt H.G., 62
Makasar Strait, 21
Mangrum, Maj Richard, 147
Manila, 136, 138, 139, 153, 154
Manila Bay, 140, 155

Manipur Valley, 89
Manterer, Maj Oscar, 169
March, Lt, 38
Maririei river, 112, 113
Markham Valley, 59
Marshall Islands, 149
Maruyama, Takeshi, 42
Massachusetts, battleship, 128
Matae, Yamakado, 42
Matupi Island, 119, 120, 121
Maungdaw-Buthidaung road, 89–90
Mavis flying-boat, 117–18
Mayu peninsula, 89
Mellet, Lt de Vaisseau, 163
Melton, Lt-Col Harry R. jnr, 92, 94
Merrill's Marauders, 82, 96, 98
Messerschmitt Bf109, 23
Meyer, Col Lyle H., 118, 150
Midway, 20, 32, 33
Mikawa, Admiral, 39
Mille Island, 149
Milne Bay, 41, 42, 44
Mims, Capt Harvey B., 4
Mindanao, 127, 131, 137, 157
Mindoro, 156
Mitchell, 'Billy', 1
Mitchell bomber, 94
Mitscher, Vice-Admiral Marc, 127, 136
Moa, corvette, 44
Mohanbari 93, 100
Montpelier, cruiser, 51
Moore, FO A., 108
Morgan, F/Sgt Keith B. 'Hank', 58
Morotai, 127
Morse, Col Winslow, 103
Mountbatten, Lord Louis, 75
Mudge, Maj-Gen Verne D., 154, 171
Munda, 40, 44, 45
Munro, F/Sgt J.K., 108
Murray, FO Jack, 57

Na-Sen, 166
Nadzab, 59, 60, 65, 69
Naf River, 89
NATO close-support aircraft, 162
Natrass, Sgt, 87
Neale, Bob, 23
Negros Island, 131
Neighbours, Lt James B., 132
New Britain, 53, 54, 59, 120, 123
New Georgia, 40, 44, 45, 149
New Guinea, 40, 48, 54, 56, 59, 60, 145
New Ireland, 35, 59, 111, 116
New Jersey, battleship, 128
Newall, ACM Sir Cyril, 17

Newcomb, Capt Sidney M., 94
Newman, Berry, 55
Newton Field, 59, 62
Ngada, 61
Nicholas, destroyer, 44
Nielson Field, 140
Ningchangyong, 95

O'Connell, Capt P.B., 102
Octans, transport, 108
Okumiya, Cdr Masatake, 37, 45, 52, 53
Olds, Bob, 52
Olson, Arvid S., 28
O'Neil, F/Sgt C.N., 121
Operation: GRATITUDE, 159
    I-GO, 44
    KA, 39, 44
    KE, 44
    NIAGARA, 171
    RO, 50
    SCOTLAND, 171
    STALEMATE II, 131
    THURSDAY, 73
Oscar, 94, 132
Owen Stanley range, 34, 41, 54
Ozawa, Admiral Jisaburo, 44, 139

P-40, 21, 22, 23, 27, 29, 89, 90
P-40B, 25, 28
P-40E, 26
P-51A Mustang, 90–104, 145
Packard, Lt 38
Palau Island, 127, 129, 130
Panay, 102
Papuan Peninsula, 35
Pearce, G/Capt C.W., 68
Pearl Harbor, 16, 19, 31, 33
Peck, Lt Walter, 7
Peleliu, 127, 136
Penniket, F/Lt J.R., 119
Pete float-plane fighter, 132
Philippine Sea, 53
Philippines 19, 20, 21, 26, 33, 127, 135, 137–9, 144–59
Philp, W/Cdr T.R., 64
Pike, FO Kenneth H., 58
Piper Cub, 62
Pittsburgh, cruiser, 142
Piva, 109–11, 124, 125
Plain of Jars, 163
Poncelet, Father R.P., 116
Port Darwin, 43
Port Moresby, 34, 41, 44, 54
Pound, Admiral of the Fleet Sir Dudley, 17

President Jackson, transport, 51
Price, F/Sgt, 114
Prince of Wales, 33
Princeton, aircraft carrier, 51

Quang Binh, 168

Rabaul, 33–53, 34, 112, 113, 149
Radar guided (SMART) bombs, 171
Radio nets, 152
Ramsden, F/Lt, 78
Ramsey, Rear-Admiral De Witte, 149
Rantan Island, 122
Raporo 36, 49, 119
Rector, Ed, 28
Red Dragon Armoured Division, 24, 31
Red River, 163, 165
Rees, Col James R., 154, 155
Rempi, 67
Repulse, 33
Reynolds, Maj Tom, 104
Richardson, Maj Elmer, 102
Rickenbaker, Maj Augustus E., 94
Riera, Lt Emmett, 139, 140
Rocket-launching tubes, 91
Rollin, Lt de Vaisseau, 164
Rouse, Lt-Col Frank, 103
Rowell, Maj-Gen Erastus 'Rusty', 5–7,
    9–11, 158
Royal Air Force, 1, 13, 72–88
Royal Australian Air Force, 55–71
Royal Flying Corps, 1, 3
Royal Naval Air Service, 3
Royal New Zealand Air Force, 105–25
Rudel, Hans Ulrich, 160
Ruff, Capt Doyle C., 168–9
Runyon, Lt Daniel, 38
Rupertus, Maj-Gen W.H., 136
Russell Island, 45, 124

SAD (Support Aircraft Direction), 152
SADE (Support Aircraft Direction
    Emergency), 152
Saidor, 64, 65
Sail Rock, 108
Sakamaki, Rear Admiral, 47
Sakhan, 7, 9
Salamaua, 54, 145
Salween gorge, 24, 26, 100, 101
San Jacinto, light carrier, 128
San Pablo, 141
Sanderson, Lt L.H., 4–5
Sante Fé, cruiser, 142
SAO (Support Aircraft Observation), 152
SAR (Support Aircraft Request), 152

Saratoga, aircraft carrier, 37, 50
Sawyer, Charley, 103
SB-3 bomber, 31
Scherger, Air Vice-Marshal F.R.W., 55,
    68, 69
Schiel, Frank, 28, 31
Scott, Col Robert L. jnr, 101
Seafire, 163
Seagrove, 106
Shaggy Ridge, 60
Shaw, destroyer, 53
Sherman, Rear-Admiral Frederick C.,
    128
Sherrod, Robert, 146
Shilling, Erik, 28
Shoemaker, Lt, 38
Simpson Harbour, 35, 117, 119, 124
Singapore, 20, 33
Sino-Japanese war, 16
Skyhawk, 167
Skyraider, 151, 159, 161, 167–72
Smith, Lt-Col A.R., 57
Smith, R.T. 'Tadpole', 28
Smoke marking, 74, 148
Sohana Island, 121
Solomon Islands, 34, 35, 39, 43, 50, 53,
    54, 147
Somerville, Sir James, 19
Sookerating, 93
South-East Asia Co-Prosperity Zone, 105
Stevens, F/Lt Louis A, 62
Stiles, Maj Wilfred, 148
Stilwell, Gen 'Vinegar Joe', 23, 73, 90, 93
Stimson, Henry, 8
Strudger, Lt, 40
Subic Bay, 21
Sulu Archipelago, 157
Sweeley, Lt Lester B., 5
Symonds, Sgt, 114

Table Bay, 42
Tachibana, Sub-Lt, 49
Talili Bay, 112, 115, 118, 123
Tan Son Nhut, 163
Tanaka, Susumu, 42
Tasman, freighter, 41
Tet offensive, 171
Thompson, S/Ldr Robert, 99
Ticonderoga, aircraft carrier, 167
Timor Sea, 145
Tingkawk Sakan, 97, 98, 100
Tobera, 36, 50, 111, 114, 121, 123
Tobruk, 32
Tojo fighter, 104
Tomahawk, 101, 103

Tonkin, Gulf of, 167
Tosbert, Joe, 103
Tourtellot, Lt 'Turk', 6
Trenchard, Lord, 1
Truk, 34, 116, 122
Tsili Tsili, 56
Tulagi, 34, 36, 37
Turner, Capt Bill, 104

Udet, Ernst, 7
Ulithi, 135
US Air Force, 167, 168
US Army Air Corps, 1, 24, 145, 146
US Army Air Force, 89, 145–6, 157
US Marine Air Groups, 144, 148
US Marine Corps, 1, 3, 4, 5, 35, 36, 106, 149, 164, 171

V2 rockets, 160
Van der Lijun, ss, 59
Vella Lavella, 48
Vietcong, 168–70
Vietminh, 165
Viggers, Lt, 111
Vila, 44
Vincent, Air Marshal, 85
Vorse, Lt A.O., 37–8
Vultee Vengeance, 19, 55–88, 145
Vunakanua, 34, 36, 49, 111, 114, 117, 120, 121, 123
Vunapope, 112, 116, 117

Waipapakauri, 106

Washington, battleship, 128
Wasp, aircraft carrier, 37
Wasp II, fleet carrier, 127, 141
Watkins, WO E.R., 79
Watson, Capt W.P., 65
Wavell, Gen, 170
Waymack, Wayne, 130
Westmoreland, Gen William C., 170
Wewak, 40
Whitehead, Maj-Gen Ennis C., 68
Widdop, H., 77
Wildcat fighter, 37
Wildebeeste torpedo-bomber, 18
Will Rogers Field, 92
Williams bridge, 86
Wingate, Maj-Gen Orde, 73, 80, 90, 91
Wirraway fighter, 19, 34
Wonam Island, 57

Ya-Na'n bridge, 86, 87
Yamada, Rear-Admiral Sadayoshi, 36
Yamamoto, Admiral Isoroku, 13, 39, 46
Yamsahita, Gen Tomoyuki, 156
Yap, 129, 135
Yellow river, 104
Yoga Yoga, 64
Yokosuka D4Y1-C 'Judy', 40
Yorktown, aircraft carrier, 26
Yunnan, 24

Zamboanga peninsula, 157
Zero 'Zeke' fighter, 22, 36, 37, 42, 51, 102, 117, 132, 134, 139